COUNTERFEIT
SILVER & GOLD

COUNTERFEIT SILVER & GOLD

How to Spot and Avoid it

By Daniel Rosenthal & Ellen Young · Silver & Gold Report

Books by Daniel M. Rosenthal:
Insider's Guide to Buying Silver & Gold—$78.00
The New Case for Silver   —$72.00
Silver & Gold Investor's Checklist   —$49.95

For further information or to order, please write
P.O. Box 40, Bethel, CT 06801.

Copyright 1984, by the SILVER & GOLD REPORT
All rights to this book are reserved. No part of this book may be used or reproduced in any manner whatsoever without written permission.
ISBN: 0-916373-01-0

Acknowledgements

Many thanks go to all the dealers and industry officials whose anecdotes, articles, comments, and (sometimes acidulous) criticisms helped pave the way for this book: James U. Blanchard, President of Blanchard & Co.; Gerald Bauman, Senior Numismatist at at Manfra, Tordella & Brookes; James Cook, President of Investment Rarities, Inc.; Jesse Cornish, Vice President of Investment Rarities and Chairman of ICTA's ethics committee; Donald C. Evans, President of the Industry Council for Tangible Assets (ICTA); David L. Ganz, General Counsel to the Professional Numismatists Guild (PNG); James Guaclides, Chairman of Western Federal Corp.; Bruce Kaplan, Vice President of A-Mark; Robert Mish, President of Mish International; Craig Rhyne, President of C. Rhyne & Associates; Harvey Stack, President of Stack's; and Luis Vigdor, Vice President of Manfra, Tordella & Brookes.

Special thanks to Carmen Accashian and Mike Ketcher for their great help in researching this Report.

Special thanks also to Muriel and Benjamin, who encouraged me -- when I was just a little boy -- as a coin collector.

Preface

When we wrote our first article on counterfeit silver and gold in the Late-December 1983 issue of our newsletter, the SILVER & GOLD REPORT, we had no idea it would be controversial. We thought the article was another good, useful "how-to" article along the lines of "How to get an extra 15.9 ounces of pure silver every time you buy 100," or SGR's ever popular "Dealer Price Surveys."

We were startled by the reaction.

On the one hand, investors loved it passionately. The headline touched a raw nerve. We had asked the question: "Are your krugerrands, maple leafs, and double eagles real or counterfeit?" Investors didn't know the answer and, of course, wanted to. We couldn't keep the recommended Density Counterfeit Detectors in stock.

On the other hand, many dealers hated the issue equally passionately. The subject touched a raw nerve there, too.

Why? Here's what we think the answer is:

"Bad for business." At the time we published our first issue on counterfeits, silver and gold had been in a 3-year bear market. Many dealers' sales had plunged 50%, 75%, and in some cases even more, from their peaks.

Many dealers were being eaten alive by their overhead. they were struggling to stay in business. They saw our warnings on bogus silver and gold as cutting into their remaining sales. The warnings were <u>bad for business</u>.

The most hated team in the silver and gold industry

The authors have a lot of sympathy for many of the dealers. We see most of them as natural allies in the struggle for a cleaner industry. More important, we view them as an indispensable tool for you, our readers. They are the key to wealth preservation in a world ruled by currency debasers.

Be that as it may, any "bad for business" argument leaves us icy cold. They would love us to beat the drums for them: "Close your eyes, roll up your pants, wade in, and buy, buy, buy."

But dealer wishes notwithstanding, the authors, and their newsletter, SILVER & GOLD REPORT, are not their mouthpiece. We're independent; we always have been and always will be. Our allegiance is to the investors, not the dealers.

Preface

Now, by no means were all the dealer complaints about our warnings self-serving. Many, including some of the dealers we most respect in the country, thought we had entirely overstated the problem of counterfeit metal.

Jim Blanchard (Blanchard & Co.); Jim Guaclides (Western Federal); Harvey Stack (Stack's); Rick Sundman (Littleton Coins); and Luis Vigdor (MTB) were just a few of them.

With so many top people in the industry telling us we were wrong, we did the logical thing -- we listened. We spoke with some of these dealers and met with others. At the same time, we intensified our own independent research.

Out of all this research, and simultaneous soul-searching, we became convinced of 3 dominant facts...

1. <u>The original article was correct in its thrust and most particulars.</u> Normal investors -- like you and the authors -- don't have a chance against a skilled counterfeiter unless you're forewarned and forearmed. Buying without the suggested precautions is like walking down a dark alley with pockets overflowing with money. You'd be asking -- no begging -- for trouble.

2. <u>We had, indeed, overstated the dangers of buying gold double eagles and, to a lesser degree, British gold sovereigns.</u> There could be no doubt that there were serious problems in buying double eagles. But, where the authors hadn't seen any way around them when

they wrote the first issue, Messrs. Blanchard and Vigdor showed us one way. Since then, we've learned a second way.

3. <u>We had entirely missed a dreadful counterfeit problem with bars</u> of silver and gold bullion, and another with uncirculated US silver dollars.

We corrected these points in a second article on counterfeits in the June 1984 issue of the SILVER & GOLD REPORT. Perhaps we were hopelessly naive, but we thought that issue would end any dealer hostility, while simultaneously portraying a vivid warning for investors.

The first phone call we received after the issue was mailed was from the vice president of a major silver and gold wholesaler. His reaction was (approximately):

> "It's great. You've corrected the error about double eagles. You have the warnings about the advertising in COIN WORLD and the WALL STREET JOURNAL. You told your readers that the density test is worthless for silver. You're right about the ANA and the PNG. The whole thing is excellent. Congratulations."

Unfortunately, that reaction proved to be isolated. You'll see direct evidence of that in our Afterword, "Industry Boiling Mad." Indeed, Chris Weber, a SILVER & GOLD REPORT Contributing Editor, and Editor of his own newsletter, INVESTMENT INSIGHTS,

Preface

recently told us...

"I see dealers who haven't agreed on anything else in their lives, and they agree about you. They hate you."

Being so widely hated is novel for the authors. Frankly, it's quite uncomfortable. The more so, since much of the hatred comes from people we respect. Sobeit.

This Special Report grew out of those two issues that stirred up such dreadful animosity. It's an updated -- and immensely expanded -- compendium of usable advice on how to spot and avoid counterfeit silver and gold. This Report -- as we show you in the Afterword -- caused bitter controversy in the industry even before it was published.

Back here in Bethel, the authors take consolation by reminding ourselves that they hate us for reasons we can be proud of. Because we tell you what no one else will dare tell you; because we pull no punches; and because we speak the truth whether or not it's "good for business."

Daniel Rosenthal
Senior Author

Ellen Young
Junior Author

September 1984
Bethel, Connecticut

Table of Contents

INTRODUCTION	....	1
	* The counterfeit problem is going to explode..............................	3
CHAPTER I:	THE HISTORY OF COUNTERFEITING.................	5
	* Hollowed out silver dollars................	6
	* "Five dollar" nickels......................	6
CHAPTER II:	THE COUNTERFEIT PROBLEM.......................	9
	* Are your krugerrands, maple leafs, and double eagles real or counterfeit?.........	9
	* An overview to the problem of counterfeit silver and gold................	10
	* Why take chances?...........................	16
	* Why a krugerrand is easier to counterfeit than a $10 bill............................	18
CHAPTER III:	IT'S ALMOST IMPOSSIBLE FOR YOU TO SPOT COUNTERFEITS VISUALLY.........................	20
	* Counterfeits of high-premium gold coins are usually made with real gold...........	21
	* Many private mints surpass the US Mint in quality..................................	22
CHAPTER IV:	THE MYTH OF THE "REPUTABLE" DEALER............	24
	* If you get stuck with bogus silver and gold, 9 chances out of 10 it will be from an honest dealer who didn't realize what he was doing........................	25
	* Dealer guarantees have very limited value..	29
CHAPTER V:	HOW TO DETECT COUNTERFEITS, A GUIDE FOR NON-SPECIALISTS................................	30
	* The three basic tests......................	32
	* The sight test.............................	32

	* The sound test..................................	34
	* The density test................................	36
	* The Density Counterfeit Detector...............	36
	* The "dreaded" tungsten counterfeit.............	38
	* Solution to: Which of these coins is real or counterfeit?........................	40
CHAPTER VI:	WHICH ARE THE RISKIEST SILVER AND GOLD INVESTMENTS?....................................	42
	* 4 guidelines for sorting out the high-risk investments......................	42
	* 7 specific How-To's for avoiding counterfeits..................................	46
	* Other useful suggestions for avoiding counterfeit silver and gold................	50
CHAPTER VII:	RISK ANALYSIS/KRUGERRANDS.......................	53
	* Some good news for investors wanting to buy krugerrands.............................	53
CHAPTER VIII:	RISK ANALYSIS/BRITISH GOLD SOVEREIGNS..........	56
	* Counterfeits broke the market in British gold sovereigns......................	56
CHAPTER IX:	RISK ANALYSIS/US GOLD DOUBLE EAGLES............	59
	* Two solutions to buying US gold double eagles safely..................................	60
CHAPTER X:	RISK ANALYSIS/OTHER GOLD INVESTMENTS...........	63
	* Austrian and Hungarian 100 coronas..........	63
	* Austrian 4 ducats..............................	64
	* Gold bars.......................................	64
	* Maple leafs....................................	65
	* Mexican 50 pesos...............................	65
	* Privately-minted gold coins.................	66
	* US gold medallions............................	67
CHAPTER XI:	RISK ANALYSIS/SILVER INVESTMENTS...............	69
	* Common-date, circulated US fractional coins...	69
	* Canadian fractional coins....................	70

TABLE OF CONTENTS

	* Privately-minted silver coins...............	70
	* Uncirculated US silver dollars............	71
	* Circulated US silver dollars..............	72
	* Silver bars...............................	72
CHAPTER XII:	SUGGESTED DEALERS............................	74
	* Dealers suggested for purchasing semi-numismatic silver and gold................	74
	* Partial listing of dealers offering the A-Mark guaranteed double eagles...........	75
	* Dealers suggested for purchasing silver and gold bullion investments..............	77
CHAPTER XIII:	THE FUTURE OUTLOOK FOR YOU, AS A SILVER AND GOLD INVESTOR............................	79
AFTERWORD:	INDUSTRY BOILING MAD: SGR WARNINGS ABOUT COUNTERFEIT SILVER AND GOLD INFURIATE MANY DEALERS AND TRADE ASSOCIATIONS................	81
	* Professional Numismatists Guild (PNG) accuses SILVER & GOLD REPORT.............	82
	* SILVER & GOLD REPORT responds to PNG.......	84
	* Investment Rarities Incorporated (IRI) attacks SILVER & GOLD REPORT..............	86
	* SILVER & GOLD REPORT responds to IRI.......	89
	* Where was Tonto?..........................	90
	* "The ethics of many dealers in the coin industry smell." -- Jim Cook, President, Investment Rarities........................	92
	* Counterfeits: Investment Rarities refutes Investment Rarities.......................	94
	* Industry Council for Tangible Assets (ICTA) attacks SILVER & GOLD REPORT.............	95
	* SILVER & GOLD REPORT responds to (ICTA)....	98
	* COIN WORLD calls counterfeit warnings unsubstantiated "rumors"..................	102
	* COIN WORLD vs. COIN WORLD.................	102
	* Who do you believe? COIN WORLD or COIN WORLD...............................	103
	* Blanchard attacks/upholds SILVER & GOLD REPORT...................................	104

xv

APPENDIX I:	AN OPEN LETTER TO ALL SILVER & GOLD DEALERS...	106
	* A disgrace................................	106
	* Shooting the messenger.....................	107
APPENDIX II:	FAKES AND FRAUDS: A REPRINT FROM "HOW TO BUY GOLD," BY TIMOTHY GREEN...................	110
	* Coins......................................	111
	* Gold bars..................................	112

Introduction

> "Faking gold coins has long been a profitable business, especially in Italy and Beirut, so that today there are millions of fake coins in circulation."
> -- Timothy Green, Author
> "How to Buy Gold" (1975)

Early in 1982, we checked out 7 silver and gold dealers we had heard rumors about. In the May and June 1982 issues of the SILVER & GOLD REPORT, we gave two of the dealers clean bills of health, and explicitly warned against investing with the other 5. The problem wasn't counterfeits, but lack of financial safeguards for the customers.

No one in the industry paid much attention. If anything, we were accused of "sensationalism," and "washing dirty linen in public."

Yet today, barely 2 years later, every single one of the 5 dealers we warned against is out of business. Total casualties: Over 30,000 investors lost some $80 million to $100 million.

Of the 2 dealers we gave clean bills of health to, both are around today...happy and prosperous.

We had the same problem with our exposé of Bullion Reserve. Outside of Howard Ruff and ourselves, everybody thought Bullion Reserve was legitimate. We published blistering warnings and our subscribers got out safe and sound.

But virtually everyone else in the industry pooh-poohed us. Bullion Reserve had wonderful credit references throughout the trade; they were a member of the prestigious Industry Council for Tangible Assets (ICTA); and they were the "flagship" North American retailer of Johnson Matthey, the great British refiner/wholesaler.

Yet, six weeks after our exposés, the owner of Bullion Reserve, Alan Saxon, committed suicide, and his company closed -- revealing a massive fraud. Mr. Saxon, in his farewell tape, specifically named Ruff's and our joint exposés as the "mortal" blow to Bullion Reserve.

Subscribers who heeded Ruff's and our warnings got out safe and sound. Unfortunately, over 20,000 non-subscribers were burned to the tune of $59 million.

Introduction

The counterfeit problem
is going to explode

Today, we have a small mountain of letters from grateful investors who were saved from those disasters.

Unfortunately, we also have a small mountain of letters from investors who weren't subscribers. They got our warnings too late. They were terrible, heart-rending letters. The people were pleading: Was there anything we could do to help them? Unfortunately, the answer was, "No." By then it was too late.

That's exactly the way it's going to be here, with counterfeits. This problem -- which is being pooh-poohed by industry figures today -- is going to explode just the way the IGBE and Bullion Reserve frauds exploded. It will be in newspapers, on TV, everywhere. That's when people will rush to their vaults to check their coins -- and that's when it will be too late.

Chapter I
The history of counterfeiting

> "From the striking of the first coin
> in the seventh century B.C., there has been
> a ceaseless struggle against the arts and
> the wiles of the counterfeiter."
> -- COIN WORLD (1984)

The profits in counterfeiting silver and gold provide such an incentive that the profession is almost as old as coinage itself.

Coins uncovered by archaeologists in Greek and Roman ruins show signs of progressive clipping. One person would get a coin, clip a little silver or gold off it, pass it on to the next person who would clip a little more, and so forth, until the coins in circulation were mere shadows of their original content.

Milling the edges of coins became common practice as a preventative. If you look at a modern quarter, you can still see the milling -- the lines on the edge -- which are a relic of the days when a quarter was 90% silver and worth clipping.

CHAPTER 1

Hollowed out silver dollars

The Chinese learned how to beat the system centuries ago. Using implements not unlike a dentist's pick, they would puncture a tiny hole in the side of a coin and ever so patiently scrape out the insides. Then, they'd refill the interior with base metals and carefully reseal the edges. To sight, the coin looked totally genuine.

In 19th century China, silver was much more the "coin of the realm" than gold. US silver dollars were particularly popular. Because of their popularity and their thickness (which made them easier to scrape out), silver dollars became a common victim of hollowing.

To detect these counterfeits, the Chinese merchant bankers would place a metal stamp (called a "chop") on each coin and hammer the seal in. If the coin rang true, the banker would put the coin back into circulation. The "chopmark" served as that banker's "Good Housekeeping Seal of Approval" for that coin. Chopmarked silver dollars are not at all uncommon, even today.

"Five dollar" nickels

In colonial America, before the silver dollar even existed,

The History of Counterfeiting

clipping and counterfeits were commonplace. One colonial copper coin even carried the legend "Value me as you please," an endearingly frank warning to would-be recipients that they had better be on their guard.

Courtesy of The Vergil M. Brand Collection, American Coins [Part II], Auction by Bowers and Merena, Inc.

In post-revolutionary America, counterfeiting continued. On May 11, 1784, Connecticut's HARTFORD COURANT warned:

"...beware of counterfeit gold dollars, dated 1782....These counterfeits appear to be very well made, and a person who is not cautious would be apt to receive them for good....The composition is supposed to be chiefly copper and antimony -- they are very brittle, and on ringing them the sound is shriller than that of good dollars."*

Another method favored by early American counterfeiters was to slit large gold coins in half, scrape out the middle, and insert a disk of platinum (which was much cheaper than gold in those days). These coins not only looked like the real thing, but they were perfect in weight, size, and ring.

Almost 100 years later, towards the beginning of modern times, there was a famous case of counterfeiting. The year was

*Source: NUMISMATIC NEWS

CHAPTER 1

1883, and the US government had just issued a beautiful new nickel, the Liberty Head. But they made a small error -- all they did to show the 5¢ denomination was to place a Roman "V" on the reverse. The 5¢ pieces were quickly snapped up, gold-plated, and passed as $5 pieces. The government later corrected the design by adding the word "cents" under the "V" -- but not before hundreds of people were fooled.

Courtesy of KAGIN'S Numismatic Auctions, Long Beach Numismatic and Philatelic Exposition.

The problem of counterfeit silver and gold has even been reflected in our movies. If you remember the old westerns, you may have wondered why the cowboys always bit their silver dollars and gold eagles. That traditional chomp was actually a quick, though somewhat unreliable, test to detect lead-based counterfeits. The lead coins were often noticeably softer to the bite.

Chapter II
The counterfeit problem

> "There will be disastrous results for people who have put a lot of money into numismatic gold. You can't tell a high technology forgery coming out of the Middle East from the real coin."
>
> -- Doug Casey, Editor
>
> INVESTING IN CRISIS (1984)

Are your krugerrands, maple leafs, and double eagles real or counterfeit?

One fringe benefit of the Bullion Reserve and International Gold Bullion Exchange bankruptcies is that hard-money investors are paying a lot more attention to making sure they get delivery of their silver and gold. But, how do you know the silver and gold you get is <u>really</u> silver and gold?

How do you know your krugerrands -- or maple leafs, or Mexican "gold" 50 pesos -- are really gold? What makes you so sure they're not gold-plated bronze, brass, lead or whatever?

CHAPTER 2

And how do you know that your "numismatic" gold double eagles, dated in the early part of the century, aren't just phonies minted last week in the Middle East?

The point is, you can't be sure, you don't know, you're at risk unless you actually check out your coins, one by one, for counterfeits. Unless you make sure your coins are genuine -- you've only gone 90% of the way.

That remaining 10% risk factor, as you'll see, is very real. There are disturbingly large numbers of counterfeits out there. Indeed, in 1982 and 1983, <u>people spent more money on counterfeit gold coins than was lost in all the bankruptcies of the silver and gold dealers combined</u>.

An overview to the problem of
counterfeit silver and gold

Here are the grim facts about counterfeit silver and gold which many dealers and trade associations wish we wouldn't publish.

1. <u>Tons of counterfeit gold coins are made each year</u>. The volume varies with the market, just like the sales of genuine gold coins. For instance, last year, with prices flat, the volume of counterfeits was between 5 and 8 tons.

The Counterfeit Problem

That 5 to 8 tons translates into hundreds of thousands of bogus coins -- for 1983 alone. The year before, the tonnage of fake gold coins -- and presumably the quantity as well -- was twice as large.

2. <u>Prices for counterfeit silver and gold coins are often quoted openly in Europe and South America</u>, there are so many of them. Sometimes there are even two-tier markets -- one price, for instance, for Mex 50's, another price for Italian-Mex 50's.

3. <u>It's legal to counterfeit silver and gold coins in some parts of the world</u>: You just can't cheat on the bullion content.

This quirk in the law directs the counterfeiters to high-premium gold coins. They can manufacture real gold counterfeits of these coins without fear of legal reprisal. The same gold that's in a krugerrand will mint a gold double eagle worth twice as much, and then some.

4. <u>It's almost impossible for you and me to spot well-struck real gold counterfeits.</u> Counterfeiters can use presses every bit as good as the US Mint's. It takes years for professional numismatists to become skilled enough to detect well-struck counterfeits. You and I, as amateurs, don't have a chance of spotting them.

An example: Ken Rutherford, who manufactures an excellent counterfeit detector which we'll discuss later, tells this interesting

CHAPTER 2

story about the quality of certain bogus British gold sovereigns...

"In March 1978, Bank Leu, Zurich, Switzerland, received a regular consignment of sovereigns, in sealed bags, from a leading London dealer. To the British dealer's great embarrassment, Bank Leu detected a large number of fakes in the consignment.

"The fake sovereigns were probably made in Beirut, Lebanon, and transported to Europe by courier. In 1977, Swiss police arrested one such courier carrying 4,400 counterfeit sovereigns. These counterfeits were so good that <u>they deceived some of London's leading bullion houses.</u>

"Even the Royal Mint (which produces the genuine sovereigns) was impressed. A Mint spokesman said, and I quote, 'It's not something we want to talk about really, but they are very good. <u>You could enlarge a picture of the counterfeit coin 30 times and you still wouldn't see the difference.</u>'" [Emphasis added.]

Those 4,400 counterfeit British gold sovereigns, picked up in just that one catch of just one courier, should give you an idea of the volume of business being done in these counterfeits, as well as the quality.

The Counterfeit Problem

5. <u>As recently as 5 years ago, counterfeit British gold sovereigns were so common, they broke the market</u>. People don't remember that gold sovereigns were once a high-premium coin. They were.

But counterfeiters flooded the market with high-quality, real-gold specimens and drove the price down to bullion levels. Today, the British gold sovereign sells at about the same premium as a 1/4-ounce krugerrand (the member of the krugerrand family closest to it in gold content).

6. <u>Gold double eagles are, today, even more exposed than British gold sovereigns were</u>. Double eagles are a high-profit, low-risk opportunity for counterfeiters.

The gold double eagles, today, are the most popular and liquid semi-numismatic gold coins in the world, just as the sovereigns used to be. Their premium, however, is over 100% -- about 3 times what it was for the sovereigns.

That makes the double eagles more than 3 times as profitable to counterfeit. Furthermore, they are popular among numismatically untrained investors who buy them in bulk without knowing how to authenticate them.

What's worse, many investors are buying the gold double eagles today because they believe the numismatic value of the

CHAPTER 2

coins will shield them from confiscation -- if and when the government ever decides to confiscate gold again.

The numismatic value probably will have a shielding effect if the coins are genuine. If, however, the coins are counterfeit, the shield will disappear like a will-o'-the-wisp. They will be liable to confiscation just like any other ordinary ingot of gold.

7. <u>The problem of counterfeit gold coins isn't limited to double eagles or numismatic gold</u>. For example, an article in BULL & BEAR showed that the problem of counterfeiting had become serious with krugerrands as early as 1980. The article read, in part...

> "Secret Service agents have traced thousands of fake krugerrands to counterfeiters in Los Angeles. The fake krugerrands have a brass core. After being struck from steel dies, the bogus krugerrands are plated in gold."

Actually, as we now know, the only thing unusual about these brass counterfeit krugerrands is the Los Angeles address. Most are manufactured in the Middle East -- with Lebanon, Syria, and Saudi Arabia the apparent main centers. Bombay, India and Milan, Italy are other apparent manufacturing centers.

The Counterfeit Problem

Until the bombs fell, Beirut (Lebanon) -- because of its free-wheeling banking community and excellent telecommunications -- was the preferred site for their manufacture. And, to this day, those high-quality, visually perfect krugerrands are still commonly called "Beirut krugerrands."

8. <u>Counterfeit uncirculated silver dollars are also murder</u>. The problem with uncirculated (BU) silver dollars is...

    (a) The common-date coins are valuable enough to be worth making quality counterfeits.

    (b) They're too cheap to have independently verified, one by one, by a source such as ANACS.

    (c) The density test is worthless for silver because it's easy to make an amalgam of lead, copper, and zinc that will pass any density test for silver in the world.

    (d) You can't even bite the coin, or drop it to test for sound, because that would damage the coin, and lower the value of a genuine specimen.

9. <u>Silver bars are even worse</u>. Because the design is

CHAPTER 2

so simple -- and because the density test is worthless for silver -- the bars are especially easy to counterfeit.

Every dealer has his or her own rituals, of varying complexity, for detecting counterfeit silver bars. But nothing we've seen has reassured us short of actually assaying the bar, and melting it down.

10. <u>Gold bars have their own problem</u>. The problem with gold bars is that they can be counterfeited by dilution with tungsten which has the same density as gold down to two decimal places.

This makes gold bars diluted with tungsten impervious to all density tests. Because of the crude -- or non-existent -- design on gold bars, tungsten-diluted gold bars will also pass all normal sight and weight tests popular at most dealers.

So how do you know your gold bars weren't diluted with tungsten? The answer is: In most cases, you don't.

Why take chances?

If you buy a TV for $400 or $500, you'll know right away if it doesn't work. And if it doesn't, you simply call up the

The Counterfeit Problem

dealer and get it fixed under the warranty. There are code numbers and "this and that" to prove where you got it from.

With krugerrands and other gold coins, it's a very different story. You buy one of them and stick it in your vault. Imagine what happens when six days later, or six months, or six years later, you go to sell it, and your would-be buyer says..."Sorry, that's a counterfeit."

That would-be buyer is SAYING he or she is sorry. But you're the one who's really FEELING it. You'll be out the purchase price of that coin -- all of it. And there will be nothing you can do about it. Picture yourself going back to the original dealer and telling him or her:

> "Three years ago, I bought 17 krugerrands from
> you. Today, I went to Joe's Silver & Gold Exchange,
> and the person there told me the coins are brass.
> I'd like my money back."

Put yourself in that original dealer's shoes for a moment. How does he or she know the krugerrands you have are those he sold you? How can he possibly take your word that they are the very same coins he sold you three years ago? You're stuck. You're out of luck.

Even worse, if you have one counterfeit, the odds are your

CHAPTER 2

whole stash of them is likely to be tainted -- filled with counterfeits. And the Secret Service may be poking around and asking you a lot of questions. Believe us -- it's more problems, more headaches, more losses than you want. Why take chances!

Why a krugerrand is easier to counterfeit than a $10 bill

Most investors don't realize how easy it is to manufacture, for example, a top-quality counterfeit krugerrand. When we tell them it's much easier -- and much more profitable -- to manufacture than a $10 bill, they stare in disbelief. In case that's your reaction, take this simple test to convince yourself.

Take out a $10 bill for a minute. Look at it closely. Better yet, get out a magnifying glass. Hamilton's portrait is fully detailed, right down to the folds in his shirt and the hairs on his head.

If you turn the bill over, you'll see even more detail. Every window in the Treasury Building is different. There are tiny cars parked outside the Treasury, and there are even people sitting in them. Miniature couples are walking hand in hand. You can even see the stripes on the American flags.

The Counterfeit Problem

Now look at a krugerrand. Not much detail compared with your $10 bill. On one side there's a simple design of a South African antelope (springbok), on the other a portrait of Paul Kruger. If you pull out your magnifying glass again, you won't see much more detail than you saw with the naked eye. The $10 bill was infinitely more intricate. The krugerrand would be far easier to counterfeit.

Which would be easier to pass -- 400 $10 bills or 10 krugerrands? Passing a counterfeit $10 bill is relatively high-risk. Very little bogus money is passed successfully today. The bills circulate quickly, and eventually pass through one or more banks where counterfeits are likely to be spotted. The Secret Service is highly effective, and, by all accounts, counterfeiters of paper money regularly get sent away to jail.

But silver and gold circulate slowly. A person typically holds on to them for years. Furthermore, people just don't expect their silver and gold to be counterfeit. So they don't check.

Now think of the profits for the counterfeiter. A person can manufacture a fine replica of a krugerrand out of base metal -- and gold-plate it -- for anywhere between $3 and $5. They can run advertisements in the newspapers and sell them direct to the public for $350 and change. Or they can sell them in bulk quantities to naive, unsuspecting dealers (fortunately, something of a dying breed) and get a few dollars less per coin. Either way, the counterfeiters get huge profits, and you're the one who may get stuck.

Chapter III
It's almost impossible for you to spot counterfeits visually

> "Counterfeits of this type are usually excellent and difficult to detect.... counterfeiters are sophisticated and produce their coins from presses every bit as good as their counterparts at the various American mints."
>
> -- David L. Ganz, Author
> "The World of Coins" (1980)

The art (business? science?) of counterfeiting is quite sophisticated. In 1965, the US government fooled the public into accepting base metal replicas of the traditional 90% silver coinage. The new sandwich coins look, feel, and weigh very much the same. So why worry about it?

Why worry about it indeed! The metallic content of the modern-day base metal replicas runs about 3¢ per dollar's worth of coins. For the traditional silver coinage, you get about $5.10 of metallic content per dollar's worth of coins. How's that for some pretty sophisticated clipping?

But the government isn't the only counterfeiter; it's just the most successful.

Photo, actual size, untouched

Is this krugerrand real or counterfeit?

It's Almost Impossible to Spot Them Visually

One clean dealer showed your senior author a mounting with about 20 gold bullion coins. The dealer then challenged him to pick out the counterfeits.

Your senior author studied the coins for several minutes and then picked out six. The dealer then said (approximately): "You're right, and you got more by sight than I did. But every single one of these coins is counterfeit."

And relying on vision is exactly how a banker in Texas got taken. He loaned a "client" $270,000. The collateral was a seemingly far more than adequate number of krugerrands. Only the krugerrands turned out to be counterfeit. They had good tone, good-strike -- but were made of brass.

Counterfeits of high-premium gold coins are usually made with real gold

---

It's enormously difficult to spot a well-struck real gold counterfeit. If a counterfeit of a gold coin is made out of base metal, it can be detected through a density test (see Chapter VI). But on semi-numismatic coins, such as gold double eagles, the premium is so high that counterfeits are usually made out of real gold.

Photo, actual size, untouched

Is this West German gold 10 deutschmark real or counterfeit?

CHAPTER 3

To check these coins you have to know the high points of the coin, like the knee on the picture of Liberty in the US St. Gaudens double eagle, or the eyebrow of the Liberty on the silver dollar. By examining it; and seeing if there's any slight wear; and if the wear doesn't match the luster of the coin; you get an idea something may be amiss.

Then you look at the feathers in the eagle; little irregularities on the rim; do the serifs on the 3rd "E" in "UNITED STATES OF AMERICA" show at a 45° angle or a 30° angle? In the date 1923, is the "9" 1/64th or 2/64ths of an inch higher than the "23"? You may think we're overstating the difficulty. But, actually, we're understating it.

Professional after professional will tell you that <u>only</u> a professional can tell the real from the counterfeit, and then only after extensive training, and even then only with a microscopic examination. Most investors like you and me -- who are not skilled professional numismatists -- don't have a chance.

Many private mints surpass
the US Mint in quality

Some dealers will tell you "Don't worry. The US Mint has coin presses with great pressures -- and no one can match their strike. Counterfeits are obvious."

Photo, actual size, untouched

Is this Hungarian 100 korona real or counterfeit?

-22-

It's Almost Impossible to Spot Them Visually

That dealer is trying too hard to sell you coins. He or she is either incredibly ignorant or flat-out lying to you.

The US Mint is like the McDonald's of minters. They do extraordinarily high volume. Given their volume, their quality is quite good.

But, just as you wouldn't go to McDonald's for filet mignon, you don't go to the US Mint for quality coins. MANY private mints do vastly better work. Indeed, the US government itself, if it wants quality work -- say for an inaugural medal -- goes to a private minter.

So, not only do some private minters equal the government in quality, many far surpass it. Franklin Mint and Medallic Arts are 2 private coiners whose issues are generally accepted as superior to government issues.

Photo, actual size, untouched

A US gold double eagle. Is it real or counterfeit?

Chapter IV
The myth of the "reputable" dealer

> "Anyone who wants to enter the coin business can open an office, buy advertising, print up a colorful brochure and become a 'numismatic advisor and counselor.'"
>
> -- Harvey Stack, President
> Stack's (1984)

To all of this, the most frequent answer we hear is: "Don't worry about counterfeits. Anyone who buys from a reputable dealer is safe." Usually, the person saying that is a dealer, and is implying that his or her firm is reputable and therefore safe.

Reputation is a good place to start. But if you stop there, you're in trouble. You're asking to get wiped out.

Think about this...in 1983, there was no silver and gold dealer in the country that enjoyed a better reputation than Bullion Reserve of North America.

> Johnson Matthey -- the great century-and-a-half old refiner/wholesaler, member of the London Gold Fix -- apparently allowed Bullion Reserve to wrap itself around the impeccable JM reputation. Never before,

The Myth of the "Reputable" Dealer

to our knowledge, had a member of the London Gold Fix allowed a North American retailer such broad-ranging use of its name.

Was Bullion Reserve reputable? God forbid, if you should have any questions about Bullion Reserve, you could call up the North American headquarters of Johnson Matthey in Toronto, and get a glowing reference. We did.

The people who relied on Bullion Reserve's great reputation are now out about $59 million. They'll be lucky to get 10¢ back on the dollar.

Bullion Reserve perpetuated its fraud by having insufficient silver and gold sitting in its vaults. Why would it be any more difficult for a "reputable" dealer to perpetuate a fraud with bogus silver and gold sitting there? Wouldn't it actually be easier?

If you get stuck with bogus silver and gold, 9 chances out of 10 it will be from an honest dealer who didn't realize what he was doing

---

Gold double eagles and krugerrands are not sold by vendors on street corners. They're sold by silver and gold dealers. So counterfeits could not be a problem without the tolerance -- witting

CHAPTER 4

or unwitting -- of the dealers.

That's a fact. But don't misunderstand us. We are NOT saying that most dealers are counterfeiters. We are saying we think that safeguards against counterfeits at many dealers have become too lax.

The authors' newsletter, SILVER & GOLD REPORT, has been in the forefront of reporting on silver and gold dealers. For that reason, we've had the good fortune to be able to take close looks at the inner workings of a fair number of leading dealers.

We think the overwhelming majority of them are good, honest people trying to do the right thing by their clients.

But good intentions are not enough. The silver and gold industry got sloppy during the late '70s and early '80s. Every Tom, Dick, and Harry, or retired shoe salesman got into the business as prices of both metals rose to the sky. Sales were too easy. In many cases, we think safeguards became too lax.

Today, we're <u>certain</u> that a skilled counterfeiter could beat the security at a great many dealers and sell them large amounts of bogus metal. We're not talking about passing $500 or $1,000 worth of bad metal. We're talking about passing $100,000, $250,000, or even half-a-million dollars of counterfeit silver and

The Myth of the "Reputable" Dealer

gold to a dealer, over the course of a year.

For example, many dealers will ship you silver dollars, krugerrands, and maple leafs in a plastic tube, sealed with a wire and cheap lead seal. When someone sells that tube back to them and they see their seal, in many cases they check the coins only if the seal has been broken. If it hasn't, the coins just go back on the shelf, the tube unopened.

That tube, which they believe in good faith contains genuine silver or gold coins will eventually be shipped -- unopened -- to a subsequent customer.

How do the dealers know that seal wasn't broken by the customer? How do they know the real coins weren't removed and replaced with bogus coins? They don't. The dealer may be shipping you bogus coins in all innocence.

That seal that they have put so much faith in costs less than a dollar. It would be infinitely easier to counterfeit than the coins inside.

At least one substantial dealer doesn't even ship the metal themselves. They contract with a third party to do it for them. We asked the dealer about safeguards the third party takes against receiving -- and subsequently reshipping -- counterfeit metal. They weren't able to tell us -- because they didn't even know.

CHAPTER 4

Another example is silver bars. Most dealers have their own "elaborate" system for checking them. They look at the bars and weigh them.

Yet a counterfeiter could cast a brick out of lead, copper, and zinc; plate it with silver; stamp the name of some refiner on it; and sell it to a dealer. It would weigh perfect and look perfect.

There's no sure way to detect a good counterfeit of a silver bar short of melting it and having the content assayed. We've only learned of one dealer who actually does this. Those who don't couldn't possibly spot a counterfeit of a silver bar. They would probably never know the difference, and, unintentionally, would pass the bogus metal on to you. You probably wouldn't know either -- unless the person you tried to sell it to spotted it. Then it would be too late.

We do not know whether or not this has already been happening. We are certain, however, that it could be happening.

The point is that the great, overwhelming majority of dealers would never knowingly pass counterfeit silver and gold along to you. But "knowingly" is the catch word.

If they don't know, they're going to pass that bogus metal along to you in all good faith. And very likely you'll be stuck.

The Myth of the "Reputable" Dealer

Dealer guarantees have very limited value

Some firms respond to questions about counterfeit silver and gold by stressing a guarantee. They will take back -- at any time -- the coins they sold you if they turn out to be counterfeit.

That's a good, constructive response. But it's not a solution.

There are two big problems with those guarantees. <u>First</u> is the duration of the firm. Most silver and gold investors buy and hold for years. Yet many dealers who started dealing even 3 years ago are now out of business. What good will the guarantee of a defunct firm do you?

<u>Second</u> is that elusive proof of purchase. Imagine returning to a dealer 3 years after you bought 40 krugerrands or 400 uncirculated silver dollars. You tell the dealer the coins turned out to be bogus and ask for your money back.

What if the dealer says: "I have pride in what I do, and those coins are obvious garbage. I couldn't sell them. You must have gotten those coins somewhere else." Under those circumstances, can you <u>prove</u> those coins were the ones you got from that dealer?

Chapter V
How to detect counterfeits, a guide for non-specialists

> "Counterfeits are a fact of life in the coin business: in Europe there are even quoted markets for both real and counterfeit sovereigns!"
>
> -- James Sinclair & Harry Schultz, Authors
>
> "How You Can Profit from Gold" (1980)

Few people realize how serious the problems surrounding counterfeits are. There's a natural tendency to pooh-pooh them and say: "Nope. That can't happen to me."

That was the way it was when the SILVER & GOLD REPORT started talking about the lack of investor safeguards at certain silver and gold dealers. People just couldn't imagine that the fine print of a contract could make such a difference. The problem was simply unreal and unbelievable.

It took three major bankruptcies -- International Gold Bullion Exchange, United Precious Metals, and Bullion Reserve -- in which tens of thousands of trusting investors lost over $100 million,

How to Detect Counterfeits

before the investing public at large began taking our warnings seriously.

The market value of the counterfeit gold coins minted each year is greater than the combined dollar losses of all three of those bankruptcies. The point is NOT that every other gold coin out there is lead with a micron thick coating of gold over it. Percentage-wise the actual number is small. The point is that there are counterfeits out there. Someone will get stuck. We guarantee it. We just don't want you to be the ones.

The problem comes back to the basic question: When you buy a gold coin, how do you know it's really gold? Of course, the dealer will tell you it's gold, but do you know it? No.

The dealer will tell you: "Don't worry about it. We've sold 27 squintillion coins, and not a single counterfeit."

Fine. Let's examine that last statement. Either the dealer did check each and every gold coin for counterfeiting or they didn't. If they didn't, then they don't know, and you better make sure yourself. If they did, then don't you think you should do as they do, not as they say? How do you know, for instance, that a clerk in the shipping room didn't palm a good coin and ship you a bogus one?

We've already seen that counterfeiting gold coins is a $100-million-a-year industry. Counterfeits of silver are almost

CHAPTER 5

as bad. Clearly then, it makes sense for you to try to protect your investment in silver and gold. If you catch even one counterfeit, you'll cover all your costs of detection and save hundreds of dollars in the bargain.

The three basic tests

There are three basic tests that will help you spot counterfeits: Sight, sound, and density. These three tests -- by themselves -- enable you to pick out some real gold counterfeits, some counterfeits of silver coins, and ALL common base metal counterfeits of gold coins.

Moreover, two of the three tests are incredibly simple. They should take just seconds per coin. We'll begin, however, with the most subjective and difficult test for an ordinary, numismatically untrained investor...

The sight test

Even if you are not a numismatist, make a habit of looking at each and every new gold coin you buy. Here are some of the major

How to Detect Counterfeits

warning signs to look for:

(A) Hazy letters. Hazy letters occur when a base metal core is electroplated.

(B) Cracked letters. Low-cost/low-quality counterfeiters do not make as good dies nor do they replace dies as often as a government mint does. Cracked letters would then be a red flag, but not a certain sign of a cheap counterfeit silver or gold coin.

(C) Off color. A refiner might make a coin planchet (blank from which the coin is stamped) with the right percent of gold (carat value), but with a different alloy. If you have nine krugerrands that look alike and one that's darker -- either the one or the nine is likely funny.*

(D) Bubbles in the surface. A cheap counterfeit. There will be plenty of other indications.

(E) A grainy surface. Many real gold counterfeits are cast rather than stamped. A characteristic of the

---

*If you've bought a set of the recent US gold medallions, you will not be able to avoid seeing different colors for different coins. Don't panic. There have been no counterfeits of these spotted yet. It's simply that the mint changed alloys, mid-series.

CHAPTER 5

casting process is a grainy surface. But you have to look really carefully to spot it. It's often not obvious.

Recommendation: A good book on visually spotting counterfeit coins is "Counterfeit Detection," published by the American Numismatic Association. It costs $7.50, and is available from the Laissez Faire Bookstore (206 Mercer St., New York, NY 10012).

The sound test

Sound is much easier to use and more reliable than sight for detecting counterfeits. The method is a variation of the ancient Chinese "chopmark" technique.

To train your ear to a reasonable level of skill should take you just five minutes. You need a common (cupro-nickel) half dollar, a silver dollar (or any of the private mintage 1-ounce silver coins), and a krugerrand (or any common, low-premium gold bullion coin). Beyond that, you need only a hard wood surface such as the top of an oak desk.

Then practice dropping the coins (on edge) one after another from about four inches up. That's high enough to give you a "thunk" (cupro-nickel), a "ring" (silver), and a "peal" (gold). But it shouldn't be high enough above the desk to inflict serious damage to either the coins or the desk.

Anyway, after no more than five minutes of practice, you'll be ready for the "backwards" test. Turn around and let a friend drop the coins for you. We'll bet that at least nine times out of ten, you'll be able to get the order correctly.

Warning: This test is for bullion coins only. Do NOT do this test with gold double eagles or any other coin with significant numismatic value. The rim will dent. Example: One day, the senior author accidentally dropped a $950 coin. When he picked it up, it was a $600 coin. The rim had been dented, lowering the condition from Choice Brilliant Uncirculated; the value was correspondingly reduced. Learn from our mistakes.

An alternative sound test for gold coins is the "ting" test. It sounds silly, but it really works. You need two coins -- krugerrands for instance. Balance one on your index finger. Hold the second in your hand and gently tap (ting) the second against the first. You should hear the first go "tinggggg," resonating like a tuning fork. You'll get the same effect, on maple leafs, only to a lesser degree because they are made of pure gold.

CHAPTER 5

The density test

This is far and away the most reliable test for base metal counterfeits of gold coins. Happily, it's also the easiest. You see, gold is significantly denser than lead, zinc, brass, bronze, and the other base metals that go into all known counterfeits. By "denser" we mean that the cubic inch of gold weighs more than a cubic inch of the other materials.

Because of gold's greater density, it's impossible to make, for instance, a gold-plated lead counterfeit krugerrand that's the same weight, diameter, and thickness as a true krugerrand. You can match two of the dimensions but not all three.

For instance, a gold-plated lead counterfeit krugerrand with the same thickness and diameter of a genuine krugerrand would be about 1/3 too light. And a lead fake krugerrand with the correct weight and diameter would be about half again too thick.

The Density Counterfeit Detector

So, how do you check density?

How to Detect Counterfeits

Fortunately, a small California company, owned by Ken Rutherford, whom we mentioned earlier, has developed an ingenious little gadget that enables you to check out each krugerrand right on the spot. It's 5-seconds simple, with no messy chemicals.

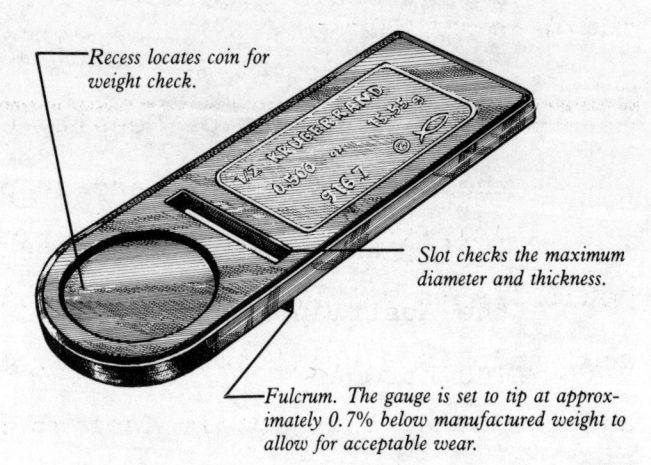

Recess locates coin for weight check.

Slot checks the maximum diameter and thickness.

Fulcrum. The gauge is set to tip at approximately 0.7% below manufactured weight to allow for acceptable wear.

The Krugerrand Density Counterfeit Detector, as we call the gadget, is a tiny balance scale with a slot in it. It checks the minimum weight and the maximum diameter/thickness of each krugerrand. You put the krugerrand on the scale and then try to push it through the slot. If the coin tilts the scale and fits through the slot, then it's gold. If it fails either test, then it's not gold. The test is that simple.

More important than mere ease, the density test <u>will spot for you every known base metal counterfeit.</u>

The Density Counterfeit Detectors come in two sets: One for the krugerrand family of gold coins, the other for all the other major gold bullion coins.

<u>Set #1</u> consists of individual Density Counterfeit Detectors to check each of the krugerrands: 1 ounce, 1/2 ounce, 1/4 ounce, 1/10 ounce, and 2 rands. The

-37-

CHAPTER 5

2-rand scale also works for British gold sovereigns.

<u>Set #2</u> consists of Density Counterfeit Detectors for the Mexican gold 50 and 20 pesos, the Canadian maple leafs, and the Austrian 100 coronas, The scale for the Austrian 100 coronas also works for the Hungarian 100 koronas.

<u>Recommendation</u>: Get whichever set or sets of Density Counterfeit Detectors suit your purchases. They will save you a lot of worry -- and potentially a lot of grief. You can buy them from the Laissez Faire Bookstore (206 Mercer St., New York, NY 10012) or direct from SGR (P.O. Box 40, Bethel, CT 06801). Either set of Density Counterfeit Detectors is $37.95. Both sets together are discounted to $70. Overseas airmail: Add $7 postage per set.

The "dreaded" tungsten counterfeit

A tungsten counterfeit is something of a bugaboo in the gold industry because it would beat the density test. You see, <u>tungsten has the same density as gold, down to two decimal places</u>.

So far, however, we've received no reports of tungsten

counterfeits. This is not surprising. Gold is soft and flows and is easy to stamp into intricate and beautiful designs. By contrast, tungsten is hard and brittle and can't be easily stamped into the designs that adorn the bullion coins.

Nevertheless, a tungsten counterfeit remains a possibility. Indeed, a subscriber phoned SGR recently and discussed possible new technology that might enable a counterfeiter to get around some of these problems.

Tungsten, by itself, would be very difficult to work with. But what if the gold content was diluted by, say, 10% tungsten? That would make it much less difficult. And, the counterfeiter could still make some decent profits from that coin. He uses $300 worth of gold, and sells the coin at spot plus 7% premium -- about $360.

But even if the tungsten counterfeit ever comes off the drawing board into practice, we suspect that the sight test will help catch it easily. Cracked letters, bubbles, blotches...you name it, we'll bet that's what you get. Even if the technology does progress to the point of eliminating the obvious problems in bogus tungsten alloys, we doubt the strike will be nearly as clear as the real thing.

And don't forget the sound test. Tungsten counterfeits may not make the same "ting" as gold, depending on the amount of dilution.

CHAPTER 5

Solution to: "Which of these coins is real or counterfeit?"

(1) 1983 krugerrand

This krugerrand is the real thing.

(2) 1973 West German gold 10 deutschmark

If you didn't catch this one, give up. We bought this "counterfeit" at the local candy shop -- a chocolate deutschmark with a gold wrapper. We made up the name "gold 10 deutschmark."

(3) 1908 Hungarian korona

This korona was also the real thing.

(4) 1884 US gold double eagle   1904 gold double eagle

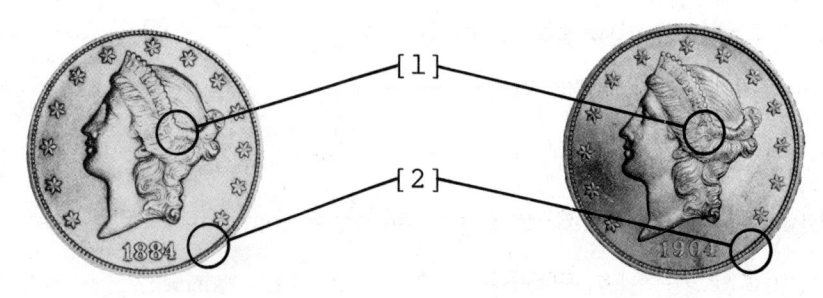

When Gerald Bauman, Senior Numismatist at Manfra, Tordella

& Brookes, first showed us this 1884 double eagle, he said it was a rather obvious fake. Many were far more subtle.

Actually the 1884 fake was subtle enough for us. How he could tell it was bogus wasn't at all obvious to us.

Then Mr. Bauman held the 1884 right up next to another double eagle, a genuine 1904 specimen. He pointed out that in comparison with the 1904 coin, the 1884 lacks sharpness of strike.

"Miss Liberty's hair detail is lacking depth of strike and all sharpness.[1] The edge reeding is wrong, lacking sharpness and being incomplete in some areas.[2] The surfaces, both obverse and reverse, are fuzzy and hazy and are slightly off color."

You can see how difficult it can be to pick out the real coins from the counterfeits. After the differences (and their significance) were pointed out to us on the double eagles, the counterfeit was obvious. But we'd be rotten, no-good liars if we said we'd have spotted the bogus double eagle on our own.

This is why so many counterfeit gold coins are impossible to spot by ordinary investors. If you don't have heavy numismatic training, you're begging to get stung -- unless you follow the precautions spelled out in this book.

Chapter VI
Which are the riskiest silver and gold investments?

"The counterfeiting of valuable coins is
a flourishing industry over much of the globe..."
-- CHANGING TIMES (1982)

Of course, some silver and gold investments are riskier than others. If you choose your purchases wisely, and follow some common-sense, simple guidelines, you can cut your risk of counterfeit silver and gold dramatically. In particular, there are four guidelines for separating the high-risk investments from the low-risk silver and gold investments.

---

4 guidelines for sorting out

the high-risk investments

---

1. <u>The bigger the bar or coin, the greater the risk of counterfeits.</u> The cost to manufacture a bogus 100-ounce bar of silver and a bogus one-ounce silver coin is essentially the same. The "bar" is "worth" about $800; the "coin" is "worth" $8. Doesn't it make more sense for a counterfeiter to manufacture the larger

item than the smaller?

The same principle works with krugerrands. A base metal counterfeit of the one-ounce krugerrand costs the same to make as the 1/10-ounce krugerrand; is safer to pass (because it's more liquid); and is worth ten times as much.

So, you would expect that the risk of getting a counterfeit one-ounce krugerrand to be much more than the risk of getting a counterfeit 1/10-ounce krugerrand. And that's exactly the case. Counterfeits of the fractional krugerrands -- except in gold coin jewelry -- are almost unheard of.

2. <u>The higher the premium over bullion, the greater the risk of real gold counterfeits</u>. When you're dealing with bullion coins that usually have premiums of 3%, 5%, and maybe 7% over bullion, there is not much profitability in counterfeiting with real gold.

Why not? All a counterfeiter stands to make on a $350 krugerrand, for example, is $24 (7% of $350) minus the cost of manufacturing. That's not a very good return, considering the risk.

However, semi-numismatic and numismatic gold coins <u>are</u> profitable to counterfeit out of real gold. A quick look at the economics will show you why:

At today's prices it costs a counterfeiter about $350

CHAPTER 6

(around $345 for the gold plus a generous $5 per coin, minting) to coin a top quality gold double eagle counterfeit with the same carat content as a genuine double eagle.

That $350 investment will give the counterfeiter an uncirculated gold "double eagle" that cannot be distinguished by an ordinary investor from the real thing. So the counterfeiter can sell it wholesale (again at current prices) for about $675 or retail for about $825. His or her profit: Between $325 and $475. Mouth-watering.

The same economics apply to the numismatic gold coins, only more dramatically. For example, a gold liberty quarter eagle (US $2.50 gold coin) has only about $50 of gold in it. But in MS 60 condition it sells for about $700. A quality real gold counterfeit will net the manufacturer about $650 -- on a mere $50 investment.

Then why is it generally understood that there are vastly more counterfeit double eagles than quarter eagles? The typical buyer of the quarter eagles is a <u>numismatic collector</u>. Passing them is a coin-by-coin business, so it's hard to get volume. And the buyer is likely to be a knowledgeable numismatic collector who will eyeball each coin carefully. So each coin is relatively high-risk to pass.

By contrast, the typical buyer of the common-date double eagles is a <u>bullion investor</u>. So passing the double eagles is a bulk business. They sell by the dozens, hundreds, or even bags.

It's easy to get volume. Furthermore, the buyers tend not to be numismatic collectors and often know little or nothing about the coins they're buying. So each sale not only yields greater profit, but is far safer as well.

3. <u>The simpler the design, the greater the risk of counterfeits</u>. US gold coins have fairly intricate, beautiful designs on both the front and back. People and birds are depicted in full detail with eyes, hair, and feathers. This fine detail makes them relatively hard to counterfeit.

The big 100-ounce and 1,000-ounce bars, by contrast, have very simple designs. Often, only the refiner's name, hallmark, and serial number are imprinted on them. So these are much easier to counterfeit.

4. <u>Gold coin jewelry is the riskiest of all purchases</u>. As we pointed out earlier, in the Middle East -- where much of the gold coin jewelry is manufactured -- it is actually <u>legal</u> to make counterfeits of foreign coins. If the caratage of the coins is correct, that's enough.

Now, if you buy gold coin jewelry, the coin is in a bezel and you can't check it for authenticity with any of the common sight, sound, and density tests. Nor can you check the edge of the coin for clipping. These are reasons why counterfeiters LOVE gold coin jewelry.

CHAPTER 6

This is NOT to say that good jewelers would dream of knowingly selling you a bogus coin jewelry piece. But unless they assemble it themselves, how do they know?

More importantly, how do you know which are the jewelers who do select the coins and assemble the jewelry themselves, and which don't? Or, to put it another way, which are the safe jewelers and which aren't? We don't know, do you?

---

7 specific How-To's for
avoiding counterfeits

These 7 common-sense Guidelines will help you avoid counterfeit silver and gold and minimize your risk of getting stuck.

1. <u>Doublecheck every gold bullion coin you buy with a Density Counterfeit Detector.</u> The overwhelming preponderance of counterfeit bullion coins are made by diluting gold content with base metals. The premium over bullion on these coins just isn't high enough to make it profitable to counterfeit them out of real gold.

In the US and Canada, you will probably be relatively safe from counterfeits if you buy your coins from a medium or major-size dealer. That's because these dealers -- when buying from the public -- often use a density test, sometimes the same Density Counterfeit

Detector that we recommend you use.

But how do you know your dealer is one of those who checks? If he or she is, how do you know he is really checking every coin? How do you know he doesn't have a corrupt employee who's passing off counterfeits to you without the boss's knowledge? How do you know that your dealer isn't actually in cahoots with a counterfeiter? The point is, you don't know. So you must recheck each coin yourself.

2. <u>On gold bullion coins, use the sight and sound tests</u>. A tungsten counterfeit of a gold coin would pass the density test. So would a krugerrand of gold diluted with 10%, 20% or even 50% tungsten. Again, tungsten has the same density as gold down to two decimal places.

We've never received any reports of tungsten counterfeits. But just because we haven't received any reports, doesn't mean they aren't around. We don't THINK they're around. But we don't KNOW it. Why take chances? The sight and sound tests will give you a good measure of protection against getting stuck with this type of counterfeit.

3. <u>Check out the gold bullion coins you already have</u>. Many dealers ship their coins in little plastic containers that are sealed with the dealer's name and identification number on the seal. If you have one of those and haven't opened it yet, do so in the presence of a notary (or at least a reliable witness). Then test the coins in the notary's presence. If any or all of the coins are counterfeit, the notary's oath will be a major help in getting a refund.

CHAPTER 6

4. <u>The closer you buy to the refiner, the safer you are from counterfeits</u>. If you buy a bar or coin from one of the great refiners ...such as Engelhard, Handy & Harman, or Johnson Matthey...it's extraordinarily unlikely that you will get a below-grade or counterfeit bar.

If, by some fluke, you did get one, we're confident the refiners would stand behind their bar. But being able to prove that your bar originated with them is the key. Needless to say, if a bogus "Engelhard" bar was really a counterfeit made in some other refinery, Engelhard isn't going to stand behind <u>that</u>. So, buy your bars as close to the original source as you can. It makes the "pedigree" easier to prove.

In particular, when you buy bars from a dealer, insist (a) on bars that came directly from the refiner; (b) that this be written on the confirmation slip; and (c) that the dealer record the refiner's name and serial number of the bar on your confirmation slip. If the bar doesn't look shiny and new, we recommend you refuse to accept it.

5. <u>Buy semi-numismatic and numismatic coins only from a clean dealer with a first-rank numismatist on staff</u>. The top numismatists are incredibly proud of their eye for coins. They would be dreadfully embarrassed to see a counterfeit coin pass through their hands onto you.

-48-

So, if you buy from a dealer with a top numismatist on staff, you will probably be quite safe from counterfeits. On page 74, we give you a partial listing of dealers we feel comfortable with.

6. <u>Always get a second opinion on semi-numismatic and numismatic purchases</u>. There are probably several thousand clean dealers out there with top-notch numismatists on staff.

The problem is, if you don't have a heavy numismatic background, how do you know who these dealers are? And if you do find one, would you know if the head numismatist left? Would the head numismatist know if a dishonest clerk in the shipping department was occasionally palming good double eagles and replacing them with high quality counterfeits?

The only way for you to be sure is to have your coins double checked by an expert. Take them to another dealer with a top numismatist and get his (or her) opinion. Or, for a small fee, send them to the American Numismatic Society's Certification Service (ANACS). Their address is 818 N. Cascade, Colorado Springs, CO 80983. The phone number is (303) 632-2646.

7. <u>If you want gold coin jewelry, supply your own gold coin</u>. Make sure you check your gold coin for counterfeiting, following our Guidelines. Buy the bezel and fittings separately.

Assemble the piece yourself, if you can. It's not really that

CHAPTER 6

difficult. But even if you can't, and have to pay a local jeweler to do it for you, you'll make sure you have real gold while saving money -- no mark-up on the coin.

Other useful suggestions for
avoiding counterfeit silver and gold

The first 7 Guidelines give you the main protections for avoiding counterfeits. Follow them, and you'll minimize your risks. Below are some other useful hints, warnings, and suggestions.

OPEN the package. Gold coins and silver dollars are usually shipped in plastic tubes, sealed tight by a cheap wire and lead seal. We are amazed at how many people never open the tubes -- usually because they don't want to break the dealer's seal.

Somehow, they think the seal gives them a measure of protection. That's totally wrong. The seal is infinitely easier to counterfeit than the coins.

Don't risk getting stuck with 20 bogus krugerrands "worth" $8,000 because you don't want to break a 35¢ seal.

The density test is worthless for silver. There are hundreds -- thousands -- of different combinations of base metals that will duplicate, exactly, the density of silver. A chemist could spend all week making up different formulations of lead, zinc, and copper that would fool any density test in the world.

For silver, all you can use without a lab analysis are the sight and sound tests. You MUST train your eyes and ears, especially when buying high premium silver coins, like the uncirculated silver dollars.

ANA membership means that a dealer has paid his dues, and nothing more. The American Numismatic Association is an educational organization open to the public and to dealers. It provides many wonderful services for hobbyists, BUT it does not pretend to police the dealers.

So, whether a dealer is or is not a member of ANA has nothing to do with the firm being clean. Indeed, we'd take it as a negative sign if a dealer bragged on his ANA membership. The way we read that, frankly, is the dealer is trying to fool unwary, would-be buyers with a meaningless "credential."

PNG membership, on the other hand, is a good sign. The Professional Numismatists Guild is a VERY selective, self-regulating organization. Membership is an unusual honor and good indicator of ethical standards. Better yet, they are willing to kick out members if those members are seen to have been unethical. So, if your dealer has a staff member who belongs to PNG, it's a good (but not infallible) sign.

CHAPTER 6

COIN WORLD and the WALL STREET JOURNAL are wonderful publications for following numismatics and finance, respectively. But, to us, neither publication monitors dealer advertising carefully enough.

The WALL STREET JOURNAL, for instance, carried heavy advertising schedules for IGBE, Premex, and United Precious Metals almost up to the bitter end. They still carry advertising for Intercomex International, The Liberty Collection, and Numismatic Guild, three dealers we do NOT recommend you buy from. So, don't let your trust of their news stories (which is well founded) spill over into trust of their advertisers (which is NOT always well founded).

NUMISMATIC NEWS, a much smaller publication than COIN WORLD, seems to us to have a tighter rein on the advertising they accept from dealers.

Minor spotting and discoloration of gold coins -- like the double eagles -- is a good sign. Often, the base metals melted into the gold alloy don't mix perfectly. Over time, the coins will tarnish (discolor slightly) in spots. Newly-minted counterfeit gold coins made of real gold haven't had the time to discolor.

-52-

Chapter VII
Risk analysis/krugerrands

"In 1978 a man approached Ray in his shop...and asked if Ray was interested in purchasing 10 Krugerrands...it turned out...the 10 pieces bore similar designs to a Krugerrand but were made of a rubbery substance. (I've heard of checks bouncing, but Krugerrands?)"

-- Mike Fuljenz, Numismatist
Blanchard & Co.
NUMISMATIC NEWS (1984)

Some good news for investors wanting to buy krugerrands

There's already been an enormous tightening of security for these coins in North America. Far more dealers are checking -- one by one -- every krugerrand that they buy.

They're using a variety of sight, sound, and density tests. The Density Counterfeit Detectors that we've repeatedly recommended

CHAPTER 7

in our newsletter, the SILVER & GOLD REPORT, are coming into widespread use among dealers. One dealer we checked out was actually using 4 sets of Detectors simultaneously.

These steps don't mean ironclad protection for you -- but they sure help. They make it far harder for a counterfeiter to pass bogus krugerrands to an unsuspecting dealer who would then unwittingly pass them along to you.

Furthermore, some dealers are now using periodic lie detector tests for shipping department employees. This increases your protection against corrupt employees who might otherwise palm good coins and ship you bogus ones.

To be sure, there are still big holes in security when you're buying krugerrands. For instance, you're at risk when buying from a lazy dealer (who doesn't check all the coins) or a corrupt dealer (who is allied with a counterfeiter).

And how do you tell one of these from a good dealer?* That's a stumper, isn't it? It worries the dickens out of the authors. That's why, when they buy krugerrands and other bullion coins, they always use the Density Counterfeit Detectors. See Chapter V for a complete explanation of the Density Counterfeit Detector.

*See our list of suggested dealers on page 74.

Risk Analysis/Krugerrands

Outside of North America, counterfeit krugerrands are more common. Buy from a reputable dealer or bank <u>and</u> check them yourself. Never buy a krugerrand from a stranger on the street, or in any here-today-gone-tomorrow setting -- stay with established dealers. In particular, follow How-To's 1, 2, and 3 in Chapter VI. If you do, you'll have a leg up.

> <u>Note</u>: Some early date krugerrands and proof krugerrands have significant numismatic premiums. These can be counterfeited profitably with real gold, just like any other numismatic gold coins. If you buy any of these, follow How-To 6.

Chapter VIII
Risk analysis/British gold sovereigns

> "One of [my clients] has a private mint in Bombay where he makes sovereigns. His sovereigns look good, but they have less gold than the real ones."
>
> -- Dr. Franz Pick (1981)

Counterfeits broke the market in British gold sovereigns

The popularity of British gold sovereigns followed the growth of the British Empire. For a century, until the mass-marketed krugerrand came along in the 1970s, it was probably the world's most popular gold coin.

Between their great popularity (which made them easy to pass) and their high premium (which made them profitable to counterfeit out of real gold), counterfeit sovereigns from the Middle East, Italy, and India flooded the market. Indeed, two well-placed industry sources gave us off-the-record estimates that, at the peak, one out of every two British gold sovereigns was counterfeit.

Risk Analysis/British Gold Sovereigns

That level of counterfeiting broke the market in British gold sovereigns, forcing the premium down to bullion levels. Since then, there has been no further real-gold counterfeiting of British gold sovereigns (as far as we know) and the existing counterfeits are being slowly removed from circulation.

One major dealer tells us that a few years ago, he was finding only 3% to 6% counterfeits in sovereigns; and today it was somewhat less. That few percent may not sound like much, but it represents tens of millions of dollars of potential losses to investors.

> Note: Most counterfeits of sovereigns were made from real gold. They will pass any density test. That's the bad news. The good news is that if you do get stuck with a real gold counterfeit, you only get stuck for the low premium. That makes your downside risk on counterfeit British gold sovereigns far less than on semi-numismatic gold coins such as the gold double eagle.

If you like the British gold sovereigns, buy the new sovereigns rather than the old. They're less interesting, but the low premium on them established by the Royal Mint drove the counterfeiters away.

You may also be safer with sovereigns that have a picture of a queen rather than a king. The counterfeiters in the Middle East

CHAPTER 8

(which is where most bogus sovereigns were manufactured) apparently didn't think a woman's face was appropriate to grace a coin -- so they specialized in the kings, not queens.

Chapter IX
Risk analysis/US gold double eagles

> "It looks like there are more double eagles advertised in uncirculated condition than were ever minted. There can't be that many around."
>
> -- Philip Cowitt, Author
> "World Currency Yearbook" (1984)

We like these beautiful coins as an investment. But we've been afraid to buy them because the gold double eagle is, today, where the British gold sovereign was 15 years ago. The combination of high premium (which makes it profitable to manufacture high-quality counterfeits with real gold) and great liquidity (which makes them easy to pass) makes these coins irresistible to high-tech counterfeiters.

We were so worried about counterfeit double eagles that in the SILVER & GOLD REPORT's Late December 1983 issue, we warned: "Do not buy US gold double eagles." Since counterfeits are made of real gold, they will pass any density test or sound test. Since they are usually very high-quality counterfeits, many of these bogus gold double eagles will pass all but the most sophisticated numismatic tests. Unless you are a highly trained numismatist,

CHAPTER 9

you'll probably find most of them impossible to spot.

So how do you buy double eagles safely? We think you *can* buy them in relative safety *if you are very careful.*

Two solutions to buying
US gold double eagles safely

Some background first:

From the 1930s to the mid-'70s, gold ownership was illegal in the US. Interest in the double eagles was centered in Europe. The great bulk of the unmelted coins flowed east to Europe; many of the remainder flowed south to Latin America.

At the end of 1974, it once again became legal to own gold in the US, and the interest shifted back home. Ironically, today, most of the gold double eagles sold in America have to be reimported from abroad. Two major importers are the wholesalers: A-Mark, in the West, and Manfra, Tordella & Brookes, in the East.

MTB has a fairly large staff of numismatists who check each double eagle as it comes in. While we haven't seen the operation at A-Mark, they tell us that they do the same. So, if you buy from a dealer who buys from MTB or (presumably) A-Mark, you should have a major measure of protection. Alternatively, if you buy from a top-notch numismatic firm, you should be relatively safe. We've listed some suggested dealers on page 74.

The second solution, a very ingenious packaging, is just now appearing on the market. The firm that created it -- A-Mark -- says the program was, in large measure, spurred by our earlier warnings. We'll let you know how the program works in just a minute. First, a little background about A-Mark that's relevant...

A-Mark, unlike most large silver and gold wholesalers, grew up out of numismatics. Their president, Mr. Markoff, was a child prodigy in numismatics many years ago. Today, he is a nationally respected professional numismatist, and member of the prestigious Professional Numismatists Guild. In addition to Mr. Markoff, A-Mark has a team of other top-notch professional numismatists on staff.

These numismatists grade each double eagle imported. The uncirculated double eagles (MS 60s) are then certified as to authenticity; individually graded in writing; secured in a sturdy, coded certificate; and then sealed in a protective, tamper-resistant package.

CHAPTER 9

A-Mark guarantees the authenticity and grading of each double eagle as long as the packaging isn't tampered with. This program is an excellent, but not perfect solution to the counterfeit double eagle problem...

(A) The packaging adds a layer of protection. But both the packaging and the coin could be counterfeited.

(B) You can't get independent authentification of the coin without destroying the packaging, and hence, the guarantee.

(C) The packaging gives you 2-sided viewing privileges. But you can't touch the coin or look at it closely the way you normally would be able to. This is not an insignificant consideration to people smitten with the beauty of the coins.

(D) The guarantee of a major wholesaler is a big protection for you. But if A-Mark goes out of business, obviously, the guarantee is worthless.

Those reservations notwithstanding, A-Mark's packaging goes a long way towards resolving our concerns about buying uncirculated double eagles. It seems to us to be one of the best, sanest, and safest ways of buying them and being reasonably assured you're getting what you paid for. See the partial list of dealers who offer A-Mark guaranteed double eagles on page 75.

Chapter X
Risk analysis/other gold investments

"...A reputable scientist, one of
their own committee members, [warned] he
could easily manufacture gold bars loaded
with 40 different impurities which,
nevertheless, could pass the ASTM tests
and be certified as pure gold ingots."

-- Jack Anderson (1981)

Austrian and Hungarian 100 coronas

Austrian and Hungarian 100 coronas are, for the same reason as krugerrands, also relatively safe from counterfeits inside the US and Canada. Again, the dealers are using the Density Counterfeit Detectors. But recheck them yourself, just to be sure.

Don't worry about real gold counterfeits, even though some do exist. All you stand to lose is the premium over spot. Since these coins are now selling very close to spot, it would cost more to check them out numismatically than the few dollars you could lose.

CHAPTER 10

> Warning: The edges on these coins are not milled, and clipping has been reported.

Austrian 4 ducats

The Austrian 4 ducat is relatively hard to counterfeit because of its thinness. They are hard to pass because of their poor liquidity. We've heard no recent reports of counterfeits.

Gold bars

Gold bars are big and simply designed. They are so crudely manufactured that a gold-plated tungsten bar -- which would have the same density as gold -- could easily be manufactured to pass the sight and weight tests, the other tests many dealers do. The ease of counterfeiting these bars -- and the sloppy controls at many dealers -- means you have to be particularly careful when you buy.

The safest way, by far, to buy gold bullion in bar form is to purchase a gold futures contract and take delivery. On the Comex a futures contract is 100 ounces. On the Chicago Board of Trade it is 33.2 ounces.

The bars you'll get will have been refined by an approved refiner; accepted as "good delivery" bars by Comex; with the imprint of an internationally known and respected firm; shipped by bonded carriers; and stored in closely monitored depositories.

If you want to buy gold bullion from a dealer, remember, you are 99.9% safe from counterfeits with a bar from one of the great refiners. Follow the procedures in How-To 4.

Maple leafs

Maple leafs, like krugerrands, are relatively safe from counterfeits in North America because of the Density Counterfeit Detectors. Indeed, we have never heard a report of a counterfeit maple leaf. Still, recheck yourself.

One minor point: Maple leafs are made of pure gold, which is softer than the regular gold coin alloy. Therefore, dropping them for the sound test will probably do some minor damage to the rim. That should not appreciably affect the value of the coin. Also, the "ting" test is not as effective.

Mexican 50 pesos

Outside the US and Canada, counterfeits of these extremely beautiful coins are fairly plentiful, especially in Central and South America. Luis Vigdor, Vice President of Manfra, Tordella

CHAPTER 10

& Brookes, tells us that in South America, there is even a two-tier market for these coins: one price for the real 50 pesos, another price for the "Made in Italy" variety.

> "...in Argentina [when] they quoted on the phone, they would say the Italian-Mexico and then Mexico. They were making a dual market there."

In the US and Canada, you are relatively safe from counterfeit Mexican 50 pesos. Again, the reason is the prevalence of the Density Counterfeit Detectors which makes passing them relatively high risk. However, you never know when a counterfeit could slip through the dealer. Recheck them yourself.

Privately-minted gold coins

Privately-minted gold coins, such as those issued by Engelhard, Gold Standard Corporation, and Monex, are probably very safe from counterfeits because you are buying very close to the source. You can buy from the issuer (in the case of Gold Standard Corporation and Monex) or one step removed from the source (in the case of Engelhard). We haven't even heard a decent rumor of a counterfeit.

It makes sense. For a counterfeiter to pass, for instance, a phony Gold Standard Corporation gold coin, they'd probably have

Risk Analysis/Other Gold Investments

to sell back to Gold Standard Corporation itself. We know of no active two-way market anywhere else. Of all places in the world, Gold Standard Corporation is where a counterfeit is most likely to be spotted.

The only risk we can think of with any of the private mintages is the unlikely possibility of the company itself issuing counterfeits. Unfortunately, there is no convenient Density Counterfeit Detector made yet to check these coins, but you can perform the sight and sound tests just as easily as for any other bullion coin.

Counterfeits from the issuing company seem unlikely. But, just to be sure, the SILVER & GOLD REPORT has purchased a small sampling of each of the most common privately-minted gold coins -- under another name, so we wouldn't get preferential treatment.

We're sending them to be assayed, and we will report the results in the SILVER & GOLD REPORT. If you'd like a complimentary copy of this issue of the SILVER & GOLD REPORT when it comes in, just send a self-addressed, stamped envelope to SGR, P.O. Box 40, Bethel, CT 06801, Attention: Gabrielle Prisco.

US gold medallions

US gold medallions are, along with the maple leaf, probably

CHAPTER 10

the safest from counterfeits of all the main gold investments. Indeed, to the best of our knowledge, these coins have never yet been counterfeited. Not only that, they are a superb gold investment offering you numismatic potential at bullion prices.*

One reason they are safer for you to buy, is that their chain of distribution is so short. Most dealers buy direct from J. Aron (the principal wholesaler for these coins). J. Aron, in turn, buys direct from the US Mint.

Finally, people are buying these coins and holding on to them. They haven't started selling them back to dealers in significant quantities. So, the coins you get are almost certain to have come straight from J. Aron to your dealer.

If you buy from one of the major clean dealers like Deak, Monex, or Western Federal, you should be quite safe. (See page 77 for dealer addresses.)

---

*See SILVER & GOLD REPORT's Special Report on US gold medallions; "A better way to own gold?" It's available from SGR for $6. Write to SGR, Attention: Gabrielle Prisco, P.O. Box 40, Bethel, CT 06801.

Chapter XI
Risk analysis/silver investments

> "Gold dollars...sovereigns and
> half-sovereigns, as well as silver coins
> were manufactured in Beirut where it is
> legal to strike counterfeit specimens
> of coins relating to foreign countries."
> -- COIN WORLD (1984)

Common-date, circulated US fractional coins

The common-date, circulated US fractional coins are our choice for the safest silver investment (in terms of downside risk) you can make in the next ten years, and the most profitable of any physical holding. They are also the silver investment safest from counterfeits. We haven't heard of any substantial problem with them.

That makes sense. The coins would have to be made and then aged to look circulated. That's a lot of time and expense (and risk) to forge a "dime" that would sell (at current prices) for less than a dollar.

CHAPTER 11

The only substantial problem we believe you might find with bags of circulated US fractional silver coins is getting a bag full of clads.

As with the krugerrands, we are amazed when we hear that people just buy a bag of coins and never open them. Again, they're risking a multi-thousand dollar investment on a 35¢ lead seal.

You don't have to count the coins one by one; simply weigh the bag. A bag of US silver coins should weigh 55 pounds (with the bag included). A silver clad bag should weigh 51 pounds. Then, open the seal and pour the coins out of the canvas bag onto a level surface. Quickly check (visually) that the coins are pre-1965 silver coins.

Canadian fractional silver coins

Canadian fractional silver coins are probably just as safe from counterfeits as their US counterparts -- maybe even more so because they are less liquid, therefore less inviting for a would-be counterfeiter.

Privately-minted silver coins

Privately-minted silver coins are quite safe from counterfeits.

-70-

As with the privately-minted gold coins, the only substantial risk is that the issuing company is diluting the metal. However, we've never heard of any such problem.

You can buy one-ounce, privately-minted silver coins from the source at Gold Standard Corporation, Monex, or Sunshine. The A-Mark and Engelhard silver coins can be bought one step away from the source.

As with privately-minted gold coins, the SILVER & GOLD REPORT has anonymously purchased a small sampling of privately-minted silver coins. We'll have them assayed and report the results in a future SILVER & GOLD REPORT. For a complimentary copy, send a self-addressed, stamped envelope to SGR, P.O. Box 40, Bethel, CT 06801, Attention: Gabrielle Prisco.

Uncirculated US silver dollars

As we pointed out earlier, uncirculated, common-date US silver dollars are murder.

So the only thing you can do is train your eyes. Buy from a top numismatic dealer or a bullion firm with a top-quality numismatist on staff. We give a list of suggested dealers on page 74.

CHAPTER 11

Circulated US silver dollars

Circulated US silver dollars are probably safer than the uncirculated ones. They'd have to be aged, making them harder to manufacture. They'd also be far less profitable because the premium is lower.

Another plus with circulated silver dollars is you can use both the sight _and_ the sound test.

Silver bars

Silver bars probably have the greatest risk of counterfeits of any of the silver investments. There is just no way to check if the bar is good without having it assayed.

As with gold bars, buying a futures contract from a major commodity exchange and taking delivery is, by far, the safest way to buy silver bullion. By and large, we'd stick with the Engelhard and Johnson Matthey hallmarks. The bars you get on the Comex and Chicago Board of Trade may not be Engelhard or Johnson Matthey -- but they will be good. They'll be from refiners that the Exchange has certified as "good delivery," and has checked out pretty much the same way they check their gold refiners.

Risk Analysis/Silver Investments

In silver bars, there is a proliferation of uncommon, unusual, and rare hallmarks that are NOT "good delivery." We don't know and don't say that these hallmarks aren't all right. We don't know, period. And since we don't know, we won't buy. We don't recommend you buy them either.

One exception we're comfortable with is the Sunshine Mining hallmark which is beginning to gain acceptance in the US. You can buy their silver, direct from the mine, in bar form through their Sunshine Bullion subsidiary.

Every dealer has his or her own elaborate rituals for detecting counterfeit silver bars. But nothing really works short of melting the bar and assaying each time. So, if you want to buy from a dealer, be sure and follow How-To 4, Chapter VI, page 48.

Chapter XII
Suggested dealers

"[If by chance, a bogus coin accidentally slipped through them to you, they'd probably] get down on their knees to get it back from you and pay you any damages because it was an honest mistake and they don't want their reputation ruined."

-- James Blanchard (1984)

Dealers suggested for purchasing semi-numismatic silver and gold

---

Blanchard & Co., 4425 W. Napoleon, Metairie, LA 70001, (800) 535-7633 or in-state (504) 456-9034

Bowers & Merena, Box 1224, Wolfeboro, NH 03894, (603) 569-5095

Deak-Perera, 630 5th Avenue, New York, NY 10111, (800) 223-5510 or in-state (212) 757-0100

Suggested Dealers

Littleton Stamp & Coin Co., 253 Union St., Littleton, NH 03561, (603) 444-5386

Manfra, Tordella & Brookes (MTB), 59 West 49th St., New York, NY 10112, (800) 535-7481 or in-state (212) 621-9502

Medlar's Coins, 220 Alamo Plaza, San Antonio, TX 78205, (512) 226-2311

Stack's, 123 West 57th St., New York, NY 10019, (212) 582-2580

Note: This is an incomplete listing. Note, also that grading and pricing policies vary SHARPLY from dealer to dealer.

Partial listing of dealers offering the A-Mark guaranteed double eagles

---

This is a partial listing only, of dealers who offer A-Mark's guaranteed double eagles. We urge you to follow the regular procedures for selecting a dealer among them. Shop for price as well as safety.

Blanchard & Co., 4425 W. Napoleon, Metairie, LA 70001, (800) 535-7633 or in-state (504) 456-9034

CHAPTER 12

Deak-Perera, 677 South Figueroa, Los Angeles, CA 90017, (800) 421-8391 or in-state (800) 252-9324

FPI Securities, P.O. Box 2400, Provo, UT 84603, (801) 224-9800

International Precious Metals Corp. (IMPC), 6451 North Federal Highway, Ft. Lauderdale, FL 33308, (800) 327-5587 or in-state (305) 491-3200

Medlar's Coins, 220 Alamo Plaza, San Antonio, TX 78205, (512) 226-2311

Republic Bullion, 1605 W. Olympic Blvd., Los Angeles, CA 90015, (213) 381-5576 or in-state (800) 762-4653

C. Rhyne & Associates, 110 Cherry St., Suite 202, Seattle, WA 98104, (800) 426-7835 or in-state (800) 542-0824

Security Pacific National Bank, available at all branches throughout California. Please check your yellow pages for your nearest branch.

Western Federal Corp., 8655 E. Via De Ventura, Suite E-155, Scottsdale, AZ 85258, (800) 528-3158 or in-state (602) 998-1000

Suggested Dealers

Dealers suggested for purchasing
silver and gold bullion investments

Here is a list of silver and gold dealers which we have confidence in at this time. We have spoken with, or met with officials from these companies and we believe the people to be honest and the firms to have good safeguards for clients. Please remember, however, that the firms listed here are not the only good dealers you can buy from. There are many more. It's just that these are the ones we know about.

Blanchard & Co., 4425 W. Napoleon, Metairie, LA 70001, (800) 535-7633 or in-state (504) 456-9034

Deak-Perera, 29 Broadway, New York, NY 10006, (800) 221-5700 or in-state (212) 635-0540

Fiscal & Monetary Services, 104 Congress St., Portsmouth, NH 03801, (800) 258-7322 or in-state (603) 431-1420

Gold Standard Corp., 1600 Genessee, Suite 260, Kansas City, MO 64102, (800) 821-5648 or in-state (816) 842-4653

Investment Rarities, Inc., 1 Appletree Square, Suite 1500, Minneapolis, MN 55420, (800) 328-1860 or in-state (612) 853-0700

CHAPTER 12

<u>Manfra, Tordella & Brookes (MTB)</u>, 59 West 49th St., New York, NY 10112, (800) 535-7481 or in-state (212) 621-9502

<u>Medlar's Coins</u>, 220 Alamo Plaza, San Antonio, TX 78205, (512) 226-2311

<u>Monex International, Ltd.</u>, 4910 Birch St., Newport Beach, CA 92660, (800) 854-3361 or in-state (800) 432-7013

<u>North American Coin & Currency, Ltd.</u>, 34 West Monroe, Phoenix, AZ 85003, (800) 528-5346 or in-state (602) 256-5200

<u>Republic Bullion</u>, 1605 West Olympic Blvd., Los Angeles, CA 90015, (800) 762-4653 or in-state (213) 381-5576

<u>Western Federal Corp.</u>, 8655 East Via De Ventura, Suite E-155, Scottsdale, AZ 85258, (800) 528-3158 or in-state (602) 998-1000

Chapter XIII
The future outlook for you, as a silver and gold investor

We predict that a year or two from now, this industry is going to be a lot safer for investors like you and us.

The dealers that we talk with are telling us that customers are coming in and demanding safeguards against counterfeits. They want their gold coins run through a Density Counterfeit Detector, right before their eyes.

That's great. The firms that pioneer investor safeguards against bogus metal will clearly have a major marketing edge in the years ahead.

The dealers that fight it are spitting in the wind. They'll go the way of the Edsel.

Either way -- the pioneers growing or the others shrinking -- you win. You won't be perfectly safe. The real world never is. But there will be solutions -- at least partial solutions -- to most of the dreadful problems about counterfeits that you and we face today.

In the meantime, with care and patience, you can invest

CHAPTER 13

quite safely. It takes a little more time and effort, but the security and peace of mind are worth it -- at least to the authors.

You will see how much it's worth when, a few years from now, you're sitting on some really nice profits. At some time or another, you'll go to cash in. Then you'll find you have real silver and gold; real coins; and very real profits.

Afterword
Industry boiling mad: *SGR* warnings about counterfeit silver and gold infuriate many dealers and trade associations

"[SGR's] exaggerated accounts [of counterfeit silver and gold], coupled with sensationalism, are an insult to the ethical standards, we as ICTA, stand for and advocate. They are a slap in the face to every knowledgeable coin dealer large or small."

-- Jesse Cornish, Vice President, Investment Rarities, and Chairman Ethics Committee, Industry Council for Tangible Assets

"I seriously doubt,..." writes David L. Ganz, General Counsel, Professional Numismatists Guild, "that a serious collector has much to worry about in terms of counterfeits...[Your information on them] is misleading at best and inaccurate in many respects."

"We dispel a rumor," editorialized COIN WORLD, "There is no truth to the rumor that there is widespread counterfeit U.S. double eagles or foreign bullion coins such as British gold sovereigns...."

AFTERWORD

Quietly, and unnoticed by most investors, there has been an impassioned -- and often bitter -- debate in the industry about counterfeit silver and gold. Many dealers and trade officials think we're dead wrong. They despise us for making public our concerns for investors.

In this special Afterword, we lift the curtain on the debate and give you the front row. We are reprinting 3 forceful letters from our critics, all of whom are reputable people in organizations we respect. We are printing our answers, as well.

The debate directly follows. Read it. Judge for yourself.

Professional Numismatists Guild accuses SGR of sensationalism and inaccuracy about counterfeit silver and gold

In this letter, David Ganz, General Counsel to the Professional Numismatist Guild, accuses SGR of sensationalism and an assortment of inaccuracies. Here, verbatim, are what we see as the key points in Mr. Ganz's attack on our position:

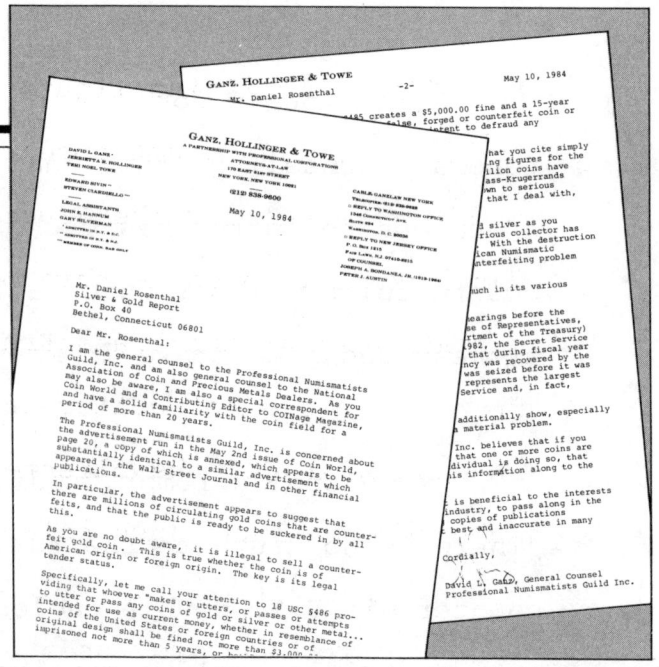

-82-

Industry Boiling Mad

"I am the general counsel to the Professional Numismatist Guild, Inc. and am also general counsel to the National Association of Coin and Precious Metals Dealers. As you may also be aware, I am also a special correspondent for Coin World and a Contributing Editor to COINage Magazine, and have a solid familiarity with the coin field for a period of more than 20 years.

"The Professional Numismatists Guild, Inc. is concerned about the advertisement run in the May 2nd issue of Coin World, page 20,...

"In particular, the advertisement appears to suggest that there are millions of circulating gold coins that are counterfeits, and that the public is ready to be suckered in by all this....

"The circulation figures and production figures that you cite simply do not appear to be accurate; the official minting figures for the Krugerrand suggest that since 1970, about 38 million coins have been produced. It seems incredible that the brass Krugerrands plated gold that you mention are not better known to serious numismatists. Certainly, in all the clientele that I deal with, I have never heard of any such coin.

"I agree that fortunes will be made in gold and silver as you suggest; I seriously doubt however, that

AFTERWORD

a serious collector has much to worry about in terms of counterfeits. With the destruction of Lebanon, and the introduction of the American Numismatic Association's Certification Service, the counterfeiting problem has all but ceased....

"We do not believe...that it is beneficial to the interests of all who are concerned with our industry, to pass along in the name of sensationalism and selling copies of publications information which is misleading at best and inaccurate in many respects.

    -- (signed: David L. Ganz
           General Counsel,
           Professional Numimatists Guild Inc.)

SGR responds to the Professional Numismatists Guild

The Professional Numismatists Guild is, in the authors' opinion, the top dealer organization in the country. It's the only one we know of that monitors its members and kicks the unethical ones out. Their General Counsel, Mr. Ganz, is a popular and respected figure in the industry.

Mr. Ganz has written an excellent book on numismatics, "The World of Coins and Coin Collecting," published in 1980.

We're sure Mr. Ganz is very proud of it. We can vouch for it, too. We enjoyed it greatly and found it full of good, meaty, useful information. We can do no better in answering PNG's accusations than to quote a few short paragraphs about counterfeits from his book:

"For the modern collector, there is perhaps no single scourge greater than that of the counterfeit coin. Particularly for those who collect gold coinage, the number of spurious specimens available for purchase is nothing short of incredible. [Emphasis added]

"...Individuals abroad who could own gold had the bullion turned into counterfeit coin, then exported it to the United States and sold it to collectors at a price far in excess of the bullion's worth.

"Counterfeits of this type are usually excellent and difficult to detect. Common and rare coins alike are the subject of this invasion; only with skill and diligence can one avoid getting stuck. [Emphasis added]

"...counterfeiters are sophisticated and produce their coins from presses every bit as good as their counterparts at the various American mints..."

-- David L. Ganz
"The World of Coins" (1980)

AFTERWORD

"I am prepared to present a counter move against SGR that entails fighting fire with fire." Jesse Cornish, Vice President of Investment Rarities

This letter is from Jesse Cornish, Vice President of Investment Rarities. It is addressed to Luis Vigdor, Vice President of Manfra, Tordella & Brookes. Both men are prominent figures in the Industry Council for Tangible Assets (ICTA).

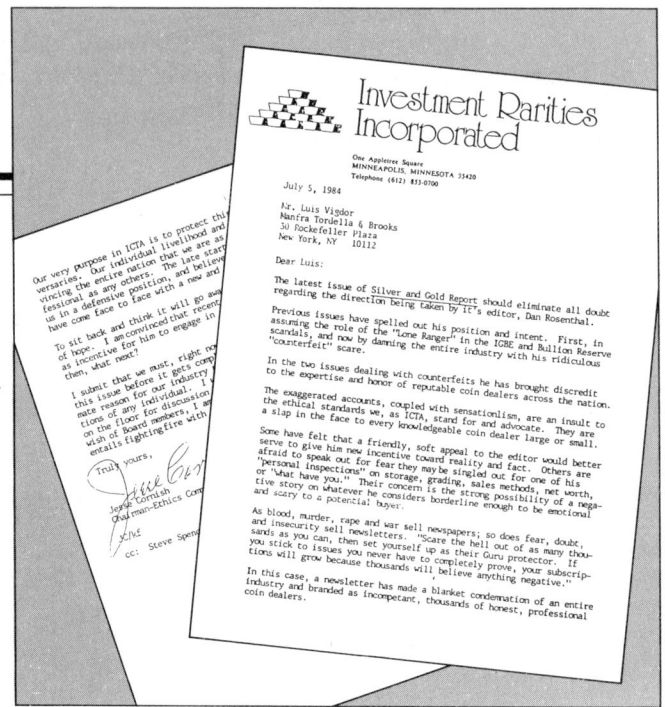

The main thrust of Mr. Cornish's letter seems to us to be a call to arms for dealers in general, and ICTA in particular, to form "battle lines" against the SILVER & GOLD REPORT. According to reports we've received, this letter was widely circulated throughout the trade. Indeed, it was a friend in the trade who sent us a copy of the letter. We quote it, in full.

"The latest issue of Silver & Gold Report should eliminate all doubt regarding the direction being taken by it's editor, Dan Rosenthal.

"Previous issues have spelled out his position and intent. First, in assuming the role of the 'Lone

-86-

Ranger' in the IGBE and Bullion Reserve scandals, and now by damning the entire industry with his ridiculous 'counterfeit' scare.

"In the two issues dealing with counterfeits he has brought discredit to the expertise and honor of reputable coin dealers across the nation.

"The exaggerated accounts, coupled with sensationalism, are an insult to the ethical standards we, as ICTA, stand for and advocate. They are a slap in the face to every knowledgeable coin dealer large or small.

"Some have felt that a friendly, soft appeal to the editor would better serve to give him new incentive toward reality and fact. Others are afraid to speak out for fear they may be singled out for one of his 'personal inspections' on storage, grading, sales methods, net worth, or 'what have you.' Their concern is the strong possibility of a negative story on whatever he considers borderline enough to be emotional and scary to a potential buyer.

"As blood, murder, rape and war sell newspapers; so does fear, doubt, and insecurity sell newsletters. 'Scare the hell out of as many thousands as you can,

AFTERWORD

then set yourself up as their Guru protector. If you stick to issues you never have to completely prove, your subscriptions will grow because thousands will believe anything negative.'

"In this case, a newsletter has made a blanket condemnation of an entire industry and branded as incompetent, thousands of honest, professional coin dealers.

"Our very purpose in ICTA is to protect this industry against all adversaries. Our individual livelihood and survival depends upon convincing the entire nation that we are as honorable, credible, and professional as any others. The late start in forming battle lines put us in a defensive position, and believe me, in this publication, we have come face to face with a new and formidable adversary.

"To sit back and think it will go away is to be lulled by the phantoms of hope. I am convinced that recent center-stage notoriety will act as incentive for him to engage in a massive direct mail campaign, and then, what next?

"I submit that we must, right now, formulate a strategy of approach to this issue before it gets completely out of hand. There is no legitimate reason for our industry to be put on trial to satiate the ambitions of any individual. I would welcome a motion to have it placed on the floor for discussion at our Detroit meeting. If it be the wish of Board members, I am prepared to present a counter move that entails fighting fire with fire."

-- (signed: Jesse Cornish
Chairman, Ethics Committee)

SGR responds to Investment Rarities

Jesse Cornish is Vice President of Investment Rarities, a silver and gold dealer that in the mid-'70s pioneered many client safeguards. Today, Investment Rarities has become one of the largest, best respected firms in the industry -- and is still probably one of the leaders in client safeguards. Mr. Cornish, like the firm he works for, is widely respected throughout the industry.

Given Mr. Cornish's position, and the stature of the firm he represents, we find it absolutely incredible that he would attack us for our great successes in exposing the IGBE and Bullion Reserve scandals.

AFTERWORD

Mr. Cornish mockingly calls the senior author "The 'Lone Ranger' in the IGBE and Bullion Reserve scandals."

Where was Tonto?

Mr. Cornish was absolutely right: We _were_ the "Lone Ranger" in those affairs....

Unfortunately, Tonto was nowhere to be seen.

SGR wrote 6 articles over 2 years exposing IGBE. How many investors were saved from the fraud, we'll never know.

What we do know is that Investment Rarities was well aware of the problem at IGBE. Jim Cook, their President, to his credit, wrote to the CFTC; BARRON'S; the WALL STREET JOURNAL; the Securities Departments of California, Florida, and Texas; and the SEC about IGBE. He got a runaround from them.

What a shame Investment Rarities didn't say in public what it was saying in private. If Mr. Cook had done what his vice president had attacked us for doing, who knows how many more investors would have been saved.

Bullion Reserve, which was a member of ICTA, is another case in point. Howard Ruff and SGR, working together, laid bare

-90-

Industry Boiling Mad

the problems at Bullion Reserve. Our articles showed probable mail fraud.

By all accounts, Ruff's articles and ours directly saved between 10,000 and 20,000 investors from getting smashed in that bankruptcy. <u>Estimated savings for Ruff's and SGR's subscribers were between $12 million and $20 million.</u>

<u>What was ICTA's reaction</u> to Ruff's warnings and ours? Did you see ICTA issue a single word of warning for investors to stay away from its member firm Bullion Reserve? We didn't.*

Even ICTA's silence, was better than Mr. Cornish's and IRI's reaction. Indeed, we received a letter from Mr. Cornish -- about our exposé -- just weeks before Bullion Reserve collapsed. In that letter, he gave the senior author what seemed like a perfunctory pat on the back, but for the most part he <u>castigated</u> us for portraying the industry in a bad light. In that letter, Mr. Cornish said...

> "The thing that disturbs me is the seemingly slanted approach to the negative....
>
> "Being 100% negative is like shooting holes in the bottom of your boat."

---

*As we went to press, ICTA's co-chairman told us that Bullion Reserve may have been kicked out before they closed, but he wasn't sure. He said he'll check it out and let us know. We'll report it in the next edition.

AFTERWORD

<u>"The ethics of many dealers in the coin industry smell."</u> -- Jim Cook, President, Investment Rarities

Let's come back now to Mr. Cornish's letter to Mr. Vigdor.

Once finished mocking SGR for successfully exposing the two largest silver and gold frauds in history, Mr. Cornish continued on the attack, saying...

> "In the two issues dealing with counterfeits, he has brought discredit to the expertise and honor of reputable coin dealers across the nation....[and] has made a blanket condemnation of an entire industry and branded as incompetent, thousands of honest, professional coin dealers."

Where Mr. Cornish got that from, we don't know. For instance, here is a quote from one of the two issues Mr. Cornish cites:

> "There are probably several thousand clean dealers out there with top-notch numismatists on staff...

> "The top numismatists are incredibly proud of their eye for coins. They would be dreadfully embarrassed to see a counterfeit coin pass through their hands on to you.

-92-

> "So, if you buy from a dealer with a top numismatist on staff, you will probably be quite safe from counterfeits."
>
> -- SGR, Mid-June, 1984

By contrast, Mr. Cornish's own firm has published blanket condemnations. For example, the notorious "Snow White & the Seven Metal Dealers." This direct-mail letter, that doubled as a full-page ad in the WALL STREET JOURNAL, attacked margin dealers, dealer storage programs, penny silver and gold mining shares, and privately-issued silver and gold coins, among other things.

That was around the turn of the year (1984). More recently, consider the article by Jim Cook, President of Investment Rarities, that appeared in the August 1984 issue of Jerome Smith's INVESTMENT PERSPECTIVES.

> "The ethics of many dealers in the coin industry smell....when Grandma brings in a silver dollar from her dresser drawer worth $500, the coin dealer thinks he was absolutely upright and shrewd when he gives her $10 for it. You can see how this morality of buying coins laps over into selling coins. If you can sell someone a ten-dollar coin for five-hundred dollars, you are not really doing anything wrong, but merely taking advantage of your superior knowledge. That's

AFTERWORD

the root cause of overgrading coins and that is why it's such a prevalent problem today. [Emphasis added]

"<u>Overgrading is the oldest and nastiest trick in the coin business.</u> It has re-emerged on a current level of sophistication that far exceeds any prior chicanery. (The entire collectible and antique industry has similar problems. <u>By my estimate, at least 75% of all collectible transactions are fraudulent either from price gouging or impaired merchandise.</u>)" [Emphasis added]

-- Jim Cook, President
Investment Rarities

<u>Counterfeits: Investment Rarities refutes Investment Rarities</u>

One of the central contentions running throughout Mr. Cornish's letter is that SGR's warnings about counterfeit silver and gold are "ridiculous."

But while Mr. Cornish, in his letter, calls our warnings about bogus metals "ridiculous," here's what his firm's advertising had to say. The excerpt is from an advertisement we received in August of '84. It is in the form of a lengthy quotation from one of the greats of the hard-money field.

Industry Boiling Mad

> "Make no mistake -- there are many areas that you should stay far away from, such as newly issued 'proof' coins peddled only to investors, high-priced rarities suitable only for expert numismatists (not amateur investors), and widely counterfeited high premium coins." [Emphasis added]

ICTA says "the buying public could be significantly injured" by SGR's warnings about counterfeit silver and gold

---

This letter, from Donald C. Evans, Jr., President of ICTA, was addressed to the NEW YORK TIMES, Department of Advertising Acceptability. In this letter, Mr. Evans accuses SGR of making "seemingly unsubstantiated and inflammatory statements."

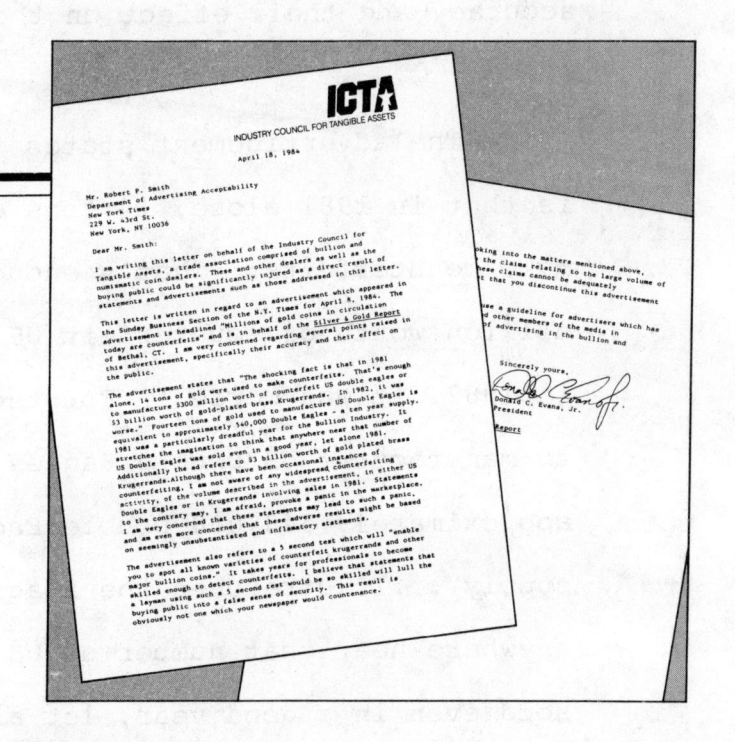

We'll begin with verbatim excerpts from Mr. Evans' letter. Then, we'll respond to what we see as Mr. Evans' key points, one by one. We want YOU to judge the validity of the factual basis of our warnings about bogus silver and gold.

-95-

AFTERWORD

"I am writing this letter on behalf of the Industry Council for Tangible Assets, a trade association comprised of bullion and numismatic coin dealers. These and other dealers as well as the buying public could be significantly injured as a direct result of the statements and advertisements such as those addressed in this letter.

"...I am very concerned regarding several points raised in this advertisement, specifically their accuracy and their effect on the public.

"The advertisement states that 'The shocking fact is that in 1981 alone, 14 tons of gold were used to make counterfeits. That's enough to manufacture $300 million worth of counterfeit US double eagles.... in 1982, it was worse.' Fourteen tons of gold used to manufacture US Double Eagles is equivalent to approximately 540,000 Double Eagles -- a ten year supply....It stretches the imagination to think that anywhere near that number of US Double Eagles was sold even in a good year, let alone 1981. Additionally the ad refers to $3 billion worth of gold plated brass Krugerrands. Although there have been occasional instances of counterfeiting, I am not aware of any widespread counterfeiting activity, of the volume described in the advertisement,

Industry Boiling Mad

....Statements to the contrary may, I am afraid, provoke a panic in the marketplace. I am...even more concerned that these adverse results might be based on seemingly unsubstantiated and inflammatory statements.

"The advertisement also refers to a 5 second test which will 'enable you to spot all known varieties of counterfeit krugerrands and other major bullion coins.' It takes years for professionals to become skilled enough to detect counterfeits. I believe that statements that a layman using such a 5 second test would be so skilled will lull the buying public into a false sense of security....

"I would appreciate your looking into the matters mentioned above, particularly with regard to the claims relating to the large volume of counterfeits in 1981. If these claims cannot be adequately substantiated I would suggest that you discontinue this advertisement until it is modified...."

-- (signed: Donald C. Evans, Jr.
President)

AFTERWORD

SILVER & GOLD REPORT responds to ICTA

The Industry Council for Tangible Assets (ICTA) is a large dealer organization representing silver and gold firms with probable combined sales of billions of dollars. ICTA has been prominent in the fight against some of the more idiotic anti-gold regulations and laws emanating from Washington and various state capitols.

We appreciate Mr. Evans' candor in sending us a copy of his letter to the NEW YORK TIMES. But, his letter certainly seems intended to disrupt our very important advantageous commercial (advertising) relationship with the NEW YORK TIMES. We regret that he didn't contact us before sending it to see if we could document our statements. As you'll now see, we can.

ICTA's first accusation: They think that the SILVER & GOLD REPORT was wrong in saying that "in 1981 alone, 14 tons were used to make counterfeits."

Our source is "Gold 1982," published by Consolidated Gold Fields. They said: "Fourteen tons of these [fake] coins were made in the Middle East during 1981."

The research reports published by Consolidated Gold Fields are the standard for professionals in the trade. They are highly regarded by everyone we've ever met in the trade.

Next, ICTA took offense at our assertion that [14 tons is] enough to manufacture $300 million worth of counterfeit US gold double eagles -- or $3 billion of gold-plated brass krugerrands."

The point we made is valid, and easy to verify by simple arithmetic. The calculations follow:

14 metric tons of gold is about 15.4 regular tons. There are about 29,000 troy ounces in a regular ton. 15.4 X 29,000 = approximately 447,000 troy ounces of gold.

Each US double eagle contains 0.9675 troy ounces of gold. Simple division then shows that you have enough gold in 447,000 troy ounces to manufacture 462,000 double eagles.

The going price for an uncirculated St. Gaudens double eagle at that time was about $900. The retail value was $900 X 462,000 = $415 million. The senior author has a dread fear of overstating his case and so conservatized his figure down to $300 million. That way, we knew the ad would be accurate even if the price of a double eagle came down sharply -- which it did.

Furthermore, using Mr. Evans' figure of 540,000 US double eagles would have made our case even stronger. Then, the retail value would have come to over $480 million, versus the $300 million we used in the ad.

AFTERWORD

A similar arithmetic process establishes the same point for gold-plated brass krugerrands.

<u>Third, ICTA objected</u> to our statement that "In 1982 [the problem of counterfeit silver and gold] was worse."

This came from "Gold 1983" issued by Consolidated Gold Fields the following year...

> "With the exception of the US, most of the medals and fake coins are fabricated in response to jewellery demand in the Middle East. Just as jewellery demand in the Middle East improved in 1982, so did the manufacture of these coins...."

<u>Fourth, our "5-second test" drew ICTA's wrath.</u> "It takes years," wrote Mr. Evans, "for professionals to become skilled enough to detect counterfeits."

Apparently, Mr. Evans inadvertently changed the context. We had been talking about bullion gold coins; he switched to semi-numismatic and numismatic gold coins.

We explicitly limited our assertions about the 5-second test to non-numismatics, i.e., to "krugerrands and other major bullion coins." These bullion coins, because of their low premiums, are normally counterfeited by a dilution of gold. Since the days of Archimedes, these have been distinguishable from the genuine coins by the mechanical means we recommend.

Indeed, <u>the means we recommend have been widely adopted by many major firms who are members of Mr. Evans' own organization, ICTA</u>.

<u>Fifth, Mr. Evans' point about semi-numismatic and numismatic coins is valid</u>. It's a point that we have stressed over and over again: The high premium coin like the US gold double eagles are normally counterfeited out of real gold. It is impossible for a regular investor like you or us to spot most of them with the naked eye.

When Mr. Evans says "It takes years for professionals to become skilled enough to detect counterfeits," he has agreed with us. This means that if you wish to invest in gold double eagles or uncirculated silver dollars, you must use safeguards such as those we recommend, or you're buying a pig in a poke.

AFTERWORD

COIN WORLD calls counterfeit warnings unsubstantiated "rumors"

COIN WORLD is one of the two leading publications of the numismatic industry (NUMISMATIC NEWS is the other). Over the years, we've recommended COIN WORLD to our readers many times.

So it was with some anguish that we read, in their May 23, 1984 issue, what we felt was a gentlemanly -- but misguided -- attack against our warnings about counterfeit silver and gold.* Then, to our amazement, we saw on the flip side of the page, an article headlined "Fake silver dollars appear."

*Although COIN WORLD didn't mention SILVER & GOLD REPORT by name, it seemed clear to all of us here in Bethel, that they meant us.

Coin World vs. Coin World

These two articles were in the same issue (May 23, 1984)
(p. 4) ... (p. 3)

We dispel a rumor ... *Fake silver dollars appear*

In their May 23, 1984 edition, *Coin World* ran an editorial, "We dispel a rumor," disputing our warnings about counterfeit silver and gold. Ironically, on the flip side of the page was an article, "Fake silver dollars appear," clearly supporting our warnings.

Note the large blow-up photographs at the bottom of the article. Those were included by *Coin World* to serve as a guide for spotting that variety of bogus silver dollar. The amount of magnification needed gives you an idea of just how hard it is, even for a numismatist, to spot bogus coins.

These two articles were both in the very next issue (May 30, 1984)
(p. 4) ... (p. 39)

To further dispel a rumor ... *Numismatic expert spots counterfeiters*

Newman tracks counterfeiters' creations

The following week *Coin World*, ironically, did the exact same thing. They ran another editorial attacking our warnings: "To further dispel a rumor." They simultaneously ran a news article "Numismatic expert spots counterfeiters," strongly supporting our warnings.

-102-

Industry Boiling Mad

The following week, there was a rerun of the confusion. Editorially, COIN WORLD again attacked our warnings* about counterfeit silver and gold -- and again ran a major news article all about how bad the problem was.

Who do you believe?
COIN WORLD or COIN WORLD?

Counterfeits are not a problem. (COIN WORLD, May 23, 1984):

> "Collectors may buy gold coins -- rare or bullion pieces -- in complete confidence today if they are dealing with established professionals. There is no truth to the rumor that there is widespread counterfeit U.S. double eagles or foreign bullion coins such as British gold sovereigns...
>
> "Fake gold (?) jewelry pieces are not rare or bullion coins and their manufacture should not be equated with the numismatic hobby or industry."**

Counterfeits are a problem. (COIN WORLD, May 30, 1984):

> "With the upsurge of interest in numismatics in

---

*See page 102.

**The quotation is printed accurately.

AFTERWORD

the early 1970s, the high prices realized for quality numismatic coins attracted the modern counterfeiter to turn his hand to antique and modern coins. Gold dollars, two-pound pieces, two-guinea and one-guinea pieces, sovereigns and half-sovereigns, as well as silver coins, were manufactured in Beirut and exported worldwide to a public hungry for material. The pieces were made quite openly in Lebanon where it is legal to strike counterfeit specimens of coins relating to foreign countries."

Blanchard attacks/upholds
SILVER & GOLD REPORT

When we wrote our first issue on counterfeit silver and gold in the SILVER & GOLD REPORT, Mr. Blanchard fired off a letter to us. It was quite a salvo -- on the one hand, explicitly upholding our "...right to inquire into these areas and make judgements..."; on the other hand, denouncing us, equally explicitly, for making several important mistakes.

Later, when Doug Casey publicly lauded our warnings on counterfeits, Mr. Blanchard fired off a letter to Mr. Casey. Again, Mr. Blanchard denounced our position as mistaken -- and, bless him, he sent us a copy of his letter.

We loved it. It's our right to research and publish what we believe to be true and relevant. It's everyone else's right to kick us in the teeth (non-violently) when we're wrong.

As it turned out, Mr. Blanchard's kicks were, for the most part, well placed. He was correct and we were wrong on some important points -- the most important being double eagles. He and Luis Vigdor convinced us there were safe ways to buy double eagles. We corrected the error in our second article on bogus metal in the SILVER & GOLD REPORT. We wish we had more critics like him.

Appendix I
An open letter to all silver and gold dealers

It is time to end efforts to suppress debate about counterfeit silver and gold

The grim truth of the matter is that when investors buy silver and gold today, they don't know what they're getting. That could rip the guts out of their entire investment strategy. It also cuts to the heart of your own industry.

Yet, instead of trying to solve the problem, many of you seem to be trying simply to shut off debate.

A disgrace

Back in December of '83, the president of a major dealer told us several horror stories about investors getting stuck with counterfeit silver and gold.

In one of them, for example, the dealer related how an investor had recently come to him with 25 gold

An Open Letter to All Silver and Gold Dealers

double eagles to sell. The coins had been purchased at another firm.

The dealer rejected the entire batch. He told us he was all but certain the whole batch was counterfeit.

That dealer, today, is publicly telling investors not to worry about counterfeits.

Shooting the messenger

Resolving the counterfeit problem is clearly in your own, enlightened, long-term self-interest. Average investors, like our subscribers, must be able to buy any reasonable silver or gold investment they want, in genuine safety from counterfeit metal. They can't now.

Yet, instead of buckling down to a free and open discussion of the problem -- the industry seems to us to be trying to suppress public debate.

Mr. Cornish, of Investment Rarities, called for "forming battle lines" against SILVER & GOLD REPORT because of its warnings about bogus metal. ICTA wrote to the NEW YORK TIMES suggesting they refuse to print our advertisement that warns about the same problem.

APPENDIX I

Further west, in Sidney, Ohio, COIN WORLD printed our ad once, then refused to rerun it. Dealer pressure? Your guess is as good as ours.

Financial Intelligence Reports won't rent us their mailing list for a direct mail letter about counterfeits "because of [the owner's] close relationship with Investment Rarities."

Even Jim Blanchard won't let us advertise our warnings about counterfeits to the subscribers of his 2 newsletters, MARKET ALERT and GOLD NEWSLETTER.

Attacking SILVER & GOLD REPORT is like the ancient custom of killing the messenger who brings bad news. It may be emotionally satisfying, but it doesn't solve the problem.

So, we're asking you to help end all efforts to suppress discussion of counterfeit silver and gold. We're not saying you, personally, or your company, is doing it. But whether or not you're doing it, it is being done -- and it's up to you and your fellow dealers to do something about it.

> Imagine the press you're going to face the very first time a substantial dealer is shown to be part of a counterfeiting ring. It will make the press surrounding the IGBE and Bullion Reserve scandals seem mild.

An Open Letter to All Silver and Gold Dealers

There will be mud on every dealer who pooh-poohed the dangers of counterfeits -- and for that matter, on every dealer who didn't. Who is going to buy silver and gold from you when the story of a $59 million counterfeit gold fraud is running on TV?

Yet, it seems obvious to us that counterfeiting silver and gold is both a relatively safe crime and an enormously profitable one. It's only a matter of time before some crook goes into the business, or some dealer who's dying on the vine turns to it.

We have one simple message for you...

"If our warnings about counterfeit silver and gold are wrong, show us. If we're wrong, we'll say so. We have no problem about admitting our errors and correcting them publicly.

"Can you say the same thing? Because, if our warnings are right, then it's up to you -- and your fellow dealers -- to take the lead in cleaning up the industry and making it safe for investors."

Until then, the issue of counterfeit silver and gold won't go away. And the SILVER & GOLD REPORT will not be silenced.

Yours sincerely,

Daniel Rosenthal

SILVER & GOLD REPORT
by Daniel Rosenthal, Editor

Appendix II
Fakes and frauds: a reprint from "How to Buy Gold," by Timothy Green

Timothy Green is a superbly knowledgeable gold insider. He knows the gold market from the mines, to the smuggling routes, to the mints and central banks. He has served as a consultant for CONSOLIDATED GOLD FIELDS and as editor of THE ILLUSTRATED LONDON NEWS. He's also a noted author and much sought-after lecturer. His books include: "The Smugglers," "The World of Gold Today," and "How to Buy Gold."

Fakes and Frauds, reprinted with permission of the publisher, Walker & Co., is a chapter from Mr. Green's "How to Buy Gold." As far back as 1975 -- when the book was first published and gold was selling for half of what it is today -- counterfeiting was already a dreadful problem. His chapter on counterfeit gold offers invaluable insight on which are the most counterfeited coins and why -- and even more important, his recommendations for buying gold safely.

Fakes and Frauds

COINS

Faking gold coins has long been a profitable business, especially in Italy and Beirut, so that today there are millions of fake coins in circulation. The forgers have turned their skill primarily towards coins like the U.S. $20 double eagle, the British sovereign, and the French 20-franc Napoleon, which command a considerable premium over their gold content. The forger's profit, in fact, comes from that premium, for many fake coins contain precisely the right amount of gold and are very hard to detect from the real thing. For this reason the faking of Austrian restrikes or the Krugerrand is less profitable, because they attract low premiums; they are not (as yet) faked much, if at all.

The best advice is to be sure to buy coins only from highly reputable dealers, who will usually inspect all coins they sell very carefully to detect fakes. In your day-to-day coin buying the coins to be most careful of are the double eagles, and the British sovereigns with the heads of Edward VII and George V (since the latter are faked in the Middle East where, for religious reasons, many people will not accept a coin with a female head). But to the uneducated eye they are hard to sort out from the real thing. So it is in your own interest to establish a good relationship with a reliable coin dealer or coin-dealing bank.

What happens if you do get stuck with some fake coins? Well, they will still probably have about the right gold content, and you should be able to sell them for their "remelt value." The price you get will be less than the gold price of the day, but at least you will not suffer a complete loss. Before selling back possible fakes for remelt value, however, be sure to check with several dealers.

GOLD BARS

The advice here is simple; buy only from first-class banks or dealers, and be sure that the bars bear the right stamps of weight, fineness, and issuer....Of course, a fake can have false details on it too, and you should never be tempted by special offers of gold bars at cut-rate prices under the prevailing gold price.

Gold dealers the world over are constantly plagued by a

APPENDIX II

number of fraudulent operators trying to sell them gold at three or four dollars an ounce under the prevailing price. These operators usually explain that the gold is part of a long-lost hoard or is the property of some South American dictator. They may even show one or two completely genuine bars in trying to con the dealers into putting up money for the rest. No doubt there will be all kinds of similar attempts to persuade the American public, newly allowed to own gold, to buy some fake bars too. So, be highly suspicious of anyone, other than an established bank or dealer, trying to sell you gold -- especially if it is a "special offer" below the day's gold price. You may think you can save money -- but you will not.

Beware also of vague newspaper or magazine advertisements offering "gold ingots" at tempting prices. There are already some cases before the courts of fraudulent companies with very fancy sounding names being set up to persuade people to buy silver bars. These companies advertised in newspapers giving P.O. Box numbers to which checks were to be mailed. They simply collected the checks and vanished into the night; they never sent an ounce of silver.

So you should be wary of newspaper advertisements. Many will be placed, of course, by entirely legitimate bullion and coin dealers and you need have no fear of dealing with them. But before mailing money to any dealer, do check out their authenticity and discuss the purchase with them by phone. And, if in doubt, ask your bank to handle the purchase of gold for you. The point is that a network of entirely trustworthy outlets is being set up...and you will save yourself both worry -- and money -- if you go directly to them.

Copyright (c) 1975. Reprinted with permission from the publisher, Walker & Co.

A message from the senior author

If you bought silver in the last 4 years, it's odds on you're losing money. And you probably don't have the faintest idea why.

Almost everyone is losing money in silver today. By the time you finish reading this letter, you're going to know why almost everyone has been losing money in silver. That's a promise. You're going to have a leg up on how you can *stop losing money in silver—and start making it again.*

The problem—and the opportunity—is this: There's been a fundamental change in the silver market that nearly everybody has missed. Your strategy for investing in silver is probably based on old information. It doesn't work anymore.

The first change is *THE GAP:* There used to be a huge shortfall—gap—between the supply of silver and the demand for it. Today the gap has become a surplus.

This graph shows the total consumption of silver minus the production of silver. As you can see, through the '70s, there was a huge gap. As you can also see, it has become a clear surplus.

The second change is *SUPPLY INELASTICITY.* This technical sounding phrase simply means that higher silver prices do NOT particularly encourage the silver mines to produce more silver. It sounds paradoxical, but it was true until 1980. The reason was that silver was mined primarily as a by-product of lead, copper, and zinc mines. The mines weren't about to dig up tons of extra lead-bearing ore to get a few dollars worth of extra silver.

Today, that's changed. The reason is that silver prices are MUCH HIGHER today than in the '70s, and lead prices aren't. So what was a few dollars of silver back then, is a major hunk of income for miners, today.

The third change is the flip side of the second: The belief that higher silver prices do NOT discourage industrial silver consumption. This was

Change #1: The Gap

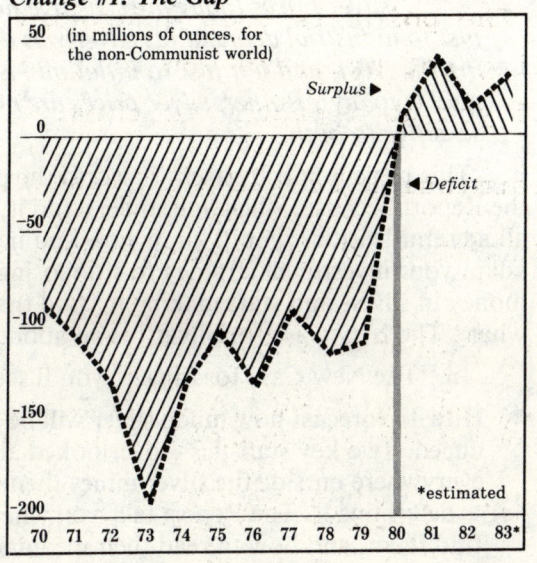

Change #2: Supply Inelasticity

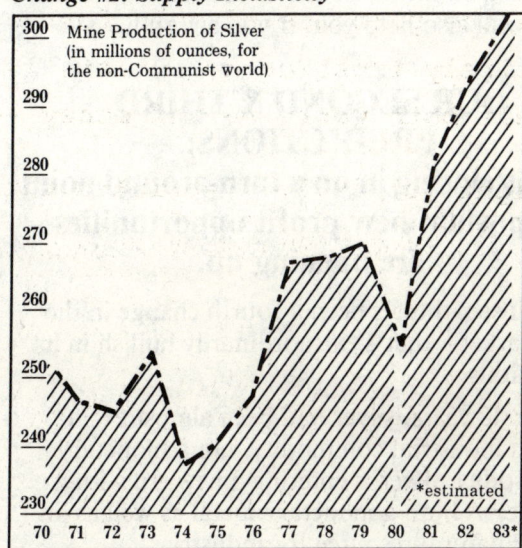

(over, please)

true until 1980. Today, it is false. Industrial consumption of silver is down 24.3% from 1979. And the decline is across the board, in almost all high-technology uses.

OUR FIRST PREDICTION:
Silver prices will go down further before heading back up

Because higher silver prices didn't encourage production or discourage consumption, the theory went that the huge gap could be filled only by dishoarding. In other words, by luring silver out of existing hoards.

Since these hoards were finite, as they declined, it would take progressively higher prices to pull the next ounce, and then the next, out of those hoards.

It was a very simple equation—back in the '70s tens—(or hundreds) of thousands of investors saw it. They invested in silver because of it. They rode prices up. They made money.

The problem is that everybody is trying to do the same thing today. And they don't understand why they're not making money anymore.

But, by now, the reason should be obvious to you. I've shown you the facts; I've fulfilled my promise to you. The reason why almost everybody is losing money in silver today is that the whole basis of their investment strategy is wrong. Finished. Kaput. Out of date.

If you think all of this, so far, sounds bearish—you're right. As I've been saying for some time in my newsletter, the *Silver & Gold Report*, I think silver is going to go down further. That's *my first prediction*. Mark it down. It's already helped my subscribers who read it a while back. It will also help you, if you act on it.

OUR SECOND & THIRD PREDICTIONS:
Silver is closing in on a turn-around point. Important new profit opportunities are opening up.

You see, there's been a fourth change in the silver market—that's extraordinarily bullish in its implications.

For 40 years, silver had been almost exclusively an industrial commodity, not a monetary metal. Today, silver is entering a new era with a dual role: as both a monetary metal as well as an essential natural resource for industry.

As a result, the dishoarding of the '60s and '70s has begun to reverse into an epic tidal wave of hoarding. As the effect of this hoarding begins to be felt in the marketplace, the bear market will grind to a halt—and then reverse. In my Special Situation Report: "The New Case for Silver," which I'll tell you about in just a minute...I explain the signs that indicate this is already beginning to come to pass. Thus, *our second prediction*: Silver is closing in on a turn-around point.

Most silver investors don't realize the enormous implications of the shift. It's one of the reasons why they are blind to the superb investment opportunities opening up in silver today.

Our third prediction: Once silver comes to that turn-around point, it's going to go back up with a vengeance. It's these dramatic shifts in the silver market that create great investment opportunities.

The fortunes are always built when everyone is looking the other way. That's the time to buy. Later, when frenzy time arrives—and it will—and everybody is rushing to get into the "choice" silver investments, you'll already be there, sitting pretty, knee-deep in profits. And that's when I'll tell you to sell and cash in.

How to get in on the ground floor of the new silver market —with information most people don't have

The *Silver & Gold Report* has just published my Special Situation Report: "The New Case for Silver." This Special Situation Report will open your eyes to what's really happening in silver today. You'll see why...

...silver prices today are sensitive not just to industrial demand (as silver was during the '70s), and not just to inflation (as gold is today). Rather, silver prices are now sensitive to both.

This basic point, by itself, is worth the price of the Report because, when you understand it, with all its ramifications, you'll know how you have to adapt your investment strategy to stop losing money in silver, and start making it. And that's what "The New Case for Silver" is all about.

In "The New Case for Silver" you'll see...

▶ **How to forecast** how much silver will be produced. Two key statistics—overlooked almost everywhere outside the silver mines themselves —determine it. The Report tells you where to find them, and how to read their meaning.

- ► **Why silver salvage** is one of the keys to predicting how low the silver market can go. What the figures are saying today.
- ► **Why coin melt** has virtually disappeared. Why that opens up a particularly interesting opportunity for conservative investors.
- ► **Why the supply of silver from India** can "perversely" decline when prices soar, and rise when prices decline. How to predict which will happen.
- ► **Why silver is far rarer** than the gold/silver price ratio would make you think...

In my second prediction, I said silver is closing in on a turn-around point. When you examine these supply statistics with us, in "The New Case for Silver" you'll see why we've been able to use them to forecast market bottoms for silver with remarkable accuracy. You'll also see where—within a narrow range—we expect the current decline to end.

For some lip-smacking profits imagine two Bunker Hunts entering the silver market at once

In "The New Case for Silver" you'll see why we flatly predict silver prices will boom again.

Do you remember, for instance, the enormous impact that Bunker Hunt had in 1979 and '80, when he bought 60 million ounces of silver? Well, in this Special Situation Report, you'll learn why a return to 8% to 13% inflation will have the same impact on the silver market as 2 Bunker Hunts. And is 8% inflation that far-fetched?

You'll also read about 2 little-discussed—but quite possible—events that could trigger a panic into silver. Or, on a more mundane level, what impact a healthy economy will have on industrial demand for silver—and silver prices. Plus...

- • **How the new currency**—which the US Treasury has already announced—will affect silver demand.
- • **Why the natural industrial substitute** for silver is...gold, which is clearly too expensive.
- • **Why the Soviet Union,** the world's second largest silver producer, has a desperate need for silver.
- • **The little-known**—but key—role Poland plays in the silver market.
- • **Where,** in a narrow range, to expect the price to bottom.
- • **What** is the equilibrium level for silver prices. What forces can alter that level up or down, and by how much.

You'll learn how to fish for the bottom of the silver market. How to ride the inflationary cycle to profits in silver. Why we expect silver to outperform gold decisively over the next decade. When you should be selling, not buying...

How you can put "The New Case for Silver" to work for you

Not all silver investments were created equal. Perhaps the nicest thing about "The New Case for Silver," is that it takes the mystery out of investing in silver. There are 14 major silver investments that you should be aware of....

Silver bullion	Private mintages
Silver call options	Numismatic silver
Mex bullion coins	Penny silver mining shares
Margin accounts	US fractional coins
Silver certificates	Canadian fractionals
US silver dollars	Silver futures
Silver put options	Blue chip mining shares

We give you a clear explanation of what each investment is...what it's designed to do...what it really can't do...who should use them...under what circumstances...and who shouldn't.

You'll see a table which spells out explicitly which investments are leveraged on the upside... which are leveraged on the downside (You'll be surprised: the two categories are not the same)...the profit potential...and overall profit/risk analyses for each.

One of the things you'll see is that one popular silver investment should be avoided by 9 out of 10 investors. On the other hand, there's a double-powered silver investment that's languishing on the sidelines, despite outstanding performance even during the down market. This second investment is simultaneously both the safest physical form of silver you can buy—and probably the one that offers the most profit potential.

You'll read about silver options: a useful new tool gaining popularity among silver investors. You'll see the right ways to use them...and the wrong ways, that cost people money...We also give you a useful comparison of the Comex, Continental Ore, Mocatta, and Monex silver options... and explain why you should avoid one of them.

You'll learn about 2 speculative investments which enable you to aim for truly exceptional

(over, please)

profits—but which also strictly limit your losses. Speaking of limiting losses...we give you the 3 cardinal rules—which most investors violate, ignore, or don't know—which enable you to limit your losses no matter what silver investments you purchase.

A rational silver investment program —profitable 81.2% of the time

In "The New Case for Silver" we particularly recommend one method for investing in silver. This method of investing is mathematically certain to shift the investment odds radically in your favor by lowering your average cost per ounce.

SGR did a computer study of the results of this silver investment program over the past 20 years. That's a time period which encompasses bear markets as well as bull. The actual results, conservatively calculated, backed up the theory... the program was profitable 81.2% of the time.

The fact that you will inevitably purchase below average retail skews the chances for profits well in your favor. It provides certainty that you will do better than what is called, in Wall Street jargon, "a random walk."

Then, after we tell you *why* and *how* this investment program works—we tell you who offers it. (We found 8 dealers—from all over the country, and one in Canada.) We polled them, and summarized the results in tabular form, so you can pick and choose at your convenience.

Send your kids to college on a modest budget

The Special Situation Report: "The New Case for Silver" is NOT for investors looking for get-rich-quick schemes. It's NOT for investors who want a list of 6 silver stocks that will double in the next 3 months. I don't have a crystal ball. I'm not a seer. I can't do that.

"The New Case for Silver" is for people who realize that silver is of enduring value and want some in their portfolio as core holdings. It's for people who might want to save to send their children to college on a modest budget. It's for people who want profits; are able to recognize an unusual opportunity—and seize upon it to help achieve their financial goals.

My personal guarantee...

There is no reason on earth you have to make the same, identical mistakes that tens of thousands of other silver investors are making. It is now completely up to you whether or not you're going to stop losing money in silver—and start making it. Give yourself a break. STOP INVESTING ON OLD, OUT-OF-DATE INFORMATION ABOUT THE SILVER MARKET.

Get the Special Situation Report: "The New Case for Silver." Examine it for a month. Show it to friends. Let your silver and gold dealers examine it too. Check out the advice, check out the data, and the analyses of the different silver investments.

Then you be the judge. At the end of the 30-day examination period, I want you to say to yourself "Yes, this Report is going to save me the shirt off my back. And, yes, it's going to show me how to make some very nice bucks in silver."

If at the end of those 30 days, you can't say those things to yourself, then I *want* that Report back from you. I think that's the best damned Report on silver available anywhere out there. I only want people who feel the same way to own it. So, if you think "The New Case for Silver" is not *everything* I've said it is, please return it for a full and prompt refund.

Warmly,

Daniel M. Rosenthal
Editor

P.S. If you'd like to subscribe to my newsletter, the *Silver & Gold Report*, "The New Case for Silver" is yours free. It's a good deal for you, and I'm happy to do it.

SILVER & GOLD REPORT, P.O. Box 40, Bethel, CT 06801

☐ Please enter my subscription to the *Silver & Gold Report*. 1 year (22 issues), Only $144. As a BONUS, I will receive "The New Case for Silver" free.

☐ I wish to purchase _____ copies of "The New Case for Silver" at a price of $72 each.

I wish to pay by: ☐ check or money order enclosed
☐ MasterCard ☐ VISA Amount $ _____

Account # _____ Exp. Date _____
Note: Tax deductible for US citizens if used for business or investment purposes.

NAME _____
ADDRESS _____
CITY/STATE/ZIP _____

Canadian and foreign subscribers may pay either in US $ or the equivalent amount in other currency. Overseas subscribers please add $20 per year for airmail postage and handling.

FREE BONUS
30-day Money-back Guarantee: Simply return the Special Report for a full, prompt refund.

CB1

FREE BONUS For a FREE sample issue of the *Silver & Gold Report*, edited by Daniel Rosenthal, return this card to:

SILVER & GOLD REPORT, P.O. Box 40, Bethel, CT USA 06801

NAME _____

ADDRESS _____

CITY/STATE/ZIP _____

FREE BONUS For a FREE sample issue of the *Silver & Gold Report*, edited by Daniel Rosenthal, return this card to:

SILVER & GOLD REPORT, P.O. Box 40, Bethel, CT USA 06801

NAME _____

ADDRESS _____

CITY/STATE/ZIP _____

FREE BONUS For a FREE sample issue of the *Silver & Gold Report*, edited by Daniel Rosenthal, return this card to:

SILVER & GOLD REPORT, P.O. Box 40, Bethel, CT USA 06801

NAME _____

ADDRESS _____

CITY/STATE/ZIP _____